THE MISSION OF BAHÁ'U'LLÁH

and other literary pieces

THE MISSION OF
BAHÁ'U'LLÁH

and other literary pieces

by

GEORGE TOWNSHEND

GR

GEORGE RONALD
Oxford

George Ronald, *Publisher*
Oxford
www.grbooks.com

ISBN 0-85398-495-6

PREFACE

THOUGH THE LITERARY pieces that make up this volume
are varied in type, they have their definite balance and
unity. They are intended to expand the personal and
devotional aspect of the Bahá'í Faith not less than the
historical.

The Genius of Ireland is the name-essay of a book now out
of print. The essay entitled *The Mission of Bahá'u'lláh* has
appeared as the Introduction to *God Passes By*[1] by Shoghi
Effendi (1944). *Nabíl's History of the Báb* was published in the
American magazine *World Order*[2]: *Queen Marie and the Bahá'í
Faith* and *The Wellspring of Happiness* in the biennial *The Bahá'í
World*[3]. Permission to reprint is gratefully acknowledged. The
poems and devotional pieces appeared (with one or two excep-
tions) in *The Altar on the Hearth* (1926). They are printed here
as being in fact a response to the first stirrings of that new spiritual
life which Bahá'u'lláh breathes in those who turn to Him, and
are in a small way a true record of the devotional approach made
by a Christian home to the realisation of the Day of God and
the acknowledgement of Bahá'u'lláh as its Lord.

The poem addressed to 'Abdu'l-Bahá, which follows
immediately, was accepted by Him in 1920.

GEORGE TOWNSHEND

Ripley,
Dundrum,
Co. Dublin,
Eire.

---

1. Bahá'í Publishing Trust, Wilmette, Illinois.
2. World Order Magazine, New York.
3. Bahá'í Publishing Trust, Wilmette, Illinois.

In his essays entitled "The Call to God" and "The Letters of 'Abdu'l-Bahá" the author has referred to the following books, in the order and the editions shown.

The Hidden Words, Bahá'u'lláh, in Arabic and Persian (Bahá'í Publishing Trust, Manchester, 1949)

Epistle to the Son of the Wolf, Bahá'u'lláh (Bahá'í Publishing Committee, Wilmette, Illinois, 1941)

Tablets of 'Abdu'l-Bahá 'Abbás, in three volumes (Bahá'í Publishing Society, Chicago, 1919)

The Bahá'í Peace Program, 'Abdu'l-Bahá (Bahá'í Publishing Committee, New York, 1930). Includes the Tablet to the Hague.

Gleanings from the Writings of Bahá'u'lláh (Bahá'í Publishing Committee, New York, 1939)

Prayers and Meditations by Bahá'u'lláh (Bahá'í Publishing Committee, New York, 1938)

CONTENTS

PART I

INTRODUCTIONS AND ESSAYS

PART II

MEDITATIONS, DEVOTIONS AND POEMS

To

BAHÁ'U'LLÁH

ONLY Beloved! With a heart on fire
And all my longings set in one desire
To make my soul a many-stringed lyre
    For Thy dear hand to play,
I bend beneath Thy mercy-seat and pray
That in the strength of perfect love I may
Tread with firm feet the red and mystic way
    Whereto my hopes aspire.

I have forgotten all for love of Thee
And ask no other joy from destiny
Than to be rapt within Thy unity
    And—whatso'er befall—
To hear no voice on earth but Thy sweet call,
To walk among Thy people as Thy thrall
And see Thy beauty breathing throughout all
    Eternal ecstasy.

Lead me forth, Lord, amid the wide world's ways,
To bear to Thee my witness and to raise
The dawn song of the breaking day of days.
    Make my whole life one flame
Of sacrificial deeds that shall proclaim
The new-born glory of Thy ancient name;
And let my death lift higher yet the same
    Triumphal chant of praise!

To

'ABDU'L-BAHÁ

HAIL to Thee, Scion of Glory, Whose utterance poureth abroad
The joy of the heavenly knowledge and the light of the greatest
of days!
Poet of mysteries chanting in rapture the beauty of God,
Unto Thee be thanksgiving and praise!

Child of the darkness that wandered in gloom but dreamed of
the light,
Lo! I have seen Thy splendour ablaze in the heavens afar
Showering gladness and glory and shattering the shadows of
night,
And seen no other star.

Thy words are to me as fragrances borne from the garden of
heaven,
Beams of a lamp that is hid in the height of a holier world,
Arrows of fire that pierce and destroy with the might of the levin
Into our midnight hurled.

Sword of the Father! none other can rend the dark veil from
my eyes,
None other can beat from my limbs with the shearing blade of
God's might
The sins I am fettered withal and give me the power to rise
And come forth to the fullness of light.

Lo! Thou hast breathed on my sorrow the sweetness of faith and
    of hope,
Thou hast chanted high paeans of joy that my heart's echoes ever
    repeat,
And the path to the knowledge of God begins to glimmer and ope
    Before my faltering feet.

Weak and unworthy my praise. Yet, as from its throbbing throat
Some lone bird pours its song to the flaming infinite sky,
So unto Thee in the zenith I lift from a depth remote
  This broken human cry.

PART I

INTRODUCTIONS AND ESSAYS

THE MISSION OF BAHÁ'U'LLÁH*

HERE IS A history of our times written on an unfamiliar theme—a history filled with love and happiness and vision and strength, telling of triumphs gained and wider triumphs yet to come: and whatever it holds of darkest tragedy it leaves mankind at its close not facing a grim inhospitable future but marching out from the shadows on the high road of an inevitable destiny towards the opened gates of the Promised City of Eternal Peace.

These hundred years as we have known them have been distinguished by human achievements and marvels unparalleled in any annals, and also by unparalleled disillusion and loss. But this history tells of wonders greater, mightier, more beneficent, wrought in the same period : and its tidings instead of tears and sorrow are of long forgotten Joy and vanished Power descended from heaven once more into the world of action and the lives of mortal men. It tells of things divine: of the birth of a new World Faith in our midst—a Faith which comes in succession to all the World Faiths of the past, acknowledging all, fulfilling all, carrying the common purpose of all to its consummation: and bearing to the Christians, "*the People of the Gospel*," a special summons to rise and help speed its propagation through the whole earth.

The narrative centres round one majestic lonely Figure, and its animating motive is the infinite transcendent love He bears for all mankind and the answering love which He draws forth from the hearts of the faithful.

The theme on its human side is that of Love and Struggle and Death. It tells of men and women like ourselves, adventuring all they had and all they were for sheer love's sake, of desolated homes, of breaking hearts, of bereavement and exile and suffering and indomitable purpose.

---

*Originally published as the introduction to *God Passes By* by Shoghi Effendi.

For long it seemed as if the world were too unhappy, too content with trivial pursuits to be able to accept in practice a Revelation so spiritual, so universal. Time and again the violent extirpation of the Faith at the hands of tyranny seemed assured. Many there were in high places in diverse lands who knew of the Faith, who were informed of the cruel wrongs inflicted on its votaries and heard their protests and appeals for justice. But there was none who heeded or who helped.

Strange and pitiful that an eager, inquiring Age which discovered so much of truth should have left the spiritual realm unexplored and should have missed the most important truth of all.

No Prophet has ever come into the world with greater proofs of His identity than Bahá'u'lláh: nor in the first century of its activity has any older Faith achieved so much or spread so far across the globe as this.

The mightiest proof of a Prophet has ever been found in Himself and in the efficacy of His word. Bahá'u'lláh rekindled the fires of faith and of happiness in the hearts of men. His knowledge was innate and spontaneous, not acquired in any school. None could gainsay or resist His wisdom and even His worst enemies admitted His greatness. All human perfections were embodied in Him. His strength was infinite. Trials and sufferings increased His firmness and power. As a divine physician He diagnosed the malady of the Age and prescribed the remedy. His teachings were universal and conferred illumination on all mankind. His power has been poured forth more abundantly since His death. In His prescience He stood alone and events have proved and are still proving its accuracy.

A second proof which every Prophet has brought with him has been the witness of the past: the evidence of Ancient Prophecy.

The fulfilment in this Day of the prophecies contained in the Qur'án and in Muslim tradition has not prevented Islám from persecuting the Bahá'í Faith but it has been startling and notorious.

The fulfilment of the prophecies of Christ and of the Bible has been over a period of a hundred years or more matter of common knowledge and remark in the West. But the full extent of that fulfilment is only seen in Bahá'u'lláh. The proclamation of His Faith was made in 1844, the year when the strict exclusion of the Jews from their own land enforced by the Muslims for some twelve centuries was at last relaxed by the Edict of Toleration and "the times of the Gentiles" were "fulfilled." The Advent has been long delayed and has fallen in a time of oppression and iniquity, of religious unreality and disbelief, when love for God and man had grown cold, when men were immersed in material business and pleasure. The Prophet came like a thief in the night and was here in our midst while people were wrapped in deep spiritual slumber. He tried and tested souls, separated the spiritual from the unspiritual, true from false believers, the sheep from the goats ; and the people taken unawares were caught as in a snare and knew not their danger till the retributive justice of God closed in upon them. Yet the appearance of the Faith and the rapidity and direction of its extension was as the lightning which flashes from the East to the West. Christianity in contrast to the Revelation of Muhammad had spread from the East to the West and has been predominantly a Western Faith. The Bahá'í Faith likewise has moved westward but with even greater speed and momentum than Christianity.

From the beginning of the Era, from the days of the Herald of the Faith, the Báb, the chronicles show a conscious sympathy of Christians with the New Teaching, which was in marked contrast with the attitude of their Muslim neighbours. The earliest instance of this, perhaps, is the kindly tribute of Dr. Cormick, an English physician resident in Tihrán, to the Báb whom he attended in prison when suffering from the effects of torture, and his record of the prevalent opinion that the teaching of the Báb resembled Christianity. The first Western historian of the Movement, Count Gobineau, a French diplomat, wrote (1865) with enthusiasm of the Báb's saintliness, of the loftiness of His ideals, of His charm, His eloquence, and of the astonishing power of His words over both friend and foe: Ernest Renan in *Les Apôtres* 1866), Lord Curzon in *Persia*, Professor Browne of Cambridge in several works, and many Christian men of letters of later date have written in a similar strain.

But among the many instances of this instinctive sympathy, the most spectacular is that which marked the execution of the Báb in the market square of Tabríz on July 9th, 1850. The officer in charge of the firing party was a Christian. He approached the Báb and prayed Him that on this account and because he had no enmity towards Him in his heart he might be spared the guilt of perpetrating so heinous a crime. The Báb replied that if his prayer were sincere God was able to fulfil his desire. The remarkable miracle by which this prayer was granted, and the martyrdom of the Báb carried out by another regiment under a Muslim officer, is a part of history.

The Christian West, though far from the scene of the Prophet's ministry, felt and responded practically to the divine World Impulse decades before the East. Poets, major and minor, Shelley and Wordsworth and many another, sang of a new Dawn. A new missionary effort spread the Christian Gospel through the earth : spiritual men and women sought to revive reality in religion : reformers arose to redress long-standing evils ; novelists used their art for a social purpose. How different all this from the action of the corrupt, fanatical, persecuting East!

The Báb Himself identified His teaching in spirit and purpose with that of Christ which was a preparation for His own: and He quoted some of Christ's instructions to His disciples as part of His own ordination address to the "Letters of the Living."

Bahá'u'lláh from the beginning seems to have realised the special capacity of the progressive and enterprising West. He took the most vigorous steps possible to bring the Truth of the Age to the knowledge of the West and its leaders. Debarred from delivering His message to Europe in person, He wrote from a Turkish prison a general Tablet to the Christians, and another Tablet to the Sovereigns and leading men of the world but especially to the rulers of Christendom: and He also addressed five personal Tablets, one to the Czar, another to the Pope, another to Queen Victoria and two to Napoleon III. In these, in ringing tones of power and majesty such as would become the

King of Kings imposing commands upon His vassals, He declared this Age the Supreme Day of God and Himself the Lord of Lords, the Father who had come in His most great glory. All that had been mentioned in the Gospel had been fulfilled. Jesus had announced this Light and His signs had been spread in the West, that His followers might in this Day set their faces towards Bahá'u'lláh.

These letters are indeed pronouncements of a far-sighted Providence: and the catastrophe of the West which has occurred since they were written gives to them now a tragic and a terrible interest. They are of some length but their drift may be generally indicated in a few paragraphs.

In His Tablet to Queen Victoria He commends Her Majesty for ending the slave trade and for "*entrusting the reins of counsel into the hands of the representatives of the people.*" But they who entered the Assembly should do so in a spirit of prayer to God and of trusteeship for the best interests of all mankind. The human race was one whole and should be regarded as the human body which though created perfect had become afflicted with grave disorders. It lay at the mercy of rulers so drunk with pride that they could not see their own best advantage, much less recognise this mighty Revelation. The one real remedy for the world's ills was the union of all its peoples in one universal Cause, one common Faith. This could be brought to pass only through the Divine Physician. He called on the Queen to ensure peace, to be just and considerate to her subjects, to avoid excessive taxation, to effect an international union for the reduction of armaments and the joint resistance of all nations to any aggressor Power.

His Tablet to the Pope contains an impassioned, loving appeal to Christians that they will recognise this, the Promised Day of God, that they will come forth into its light and acclaim their Lord, and enter the Kingdom in His name. They were created for the light and He likes not to see them in the darkness. Christ purified the world with Love and with the Spirit that in this Day it might be able to receive Life at the hands of the Merciful. This is the coming of the Father of whom Isaiah spoke: the teaching which He now reveals is that which Christ withheld when He said, "*other things I have to say unto you but ye cannot bear them now.*" He bids the Pontiff take the Cup of Life and drink therefrom and "*offer it then to such as turn towards it amongst the peoples of all Faiths.*"

The Tablet to Alexander II is in answer to a prayer addressed by the Czar to His Lord and in recognition of a kindness shown to Bahá'u'lláh when in prison and in chains by an ambassador of the Czar. He impresses on the Czar the supreme greatness of this Manifestation, tells him how the Prophet has subjected Himself to a thousand calamities for the salvation of the world and, having brought life to men, is threatened by them with death. He bids him expose this injustice, and in love for God and God's kingdom offer himself as a ransom in God's path: no harm will come to him but a reward in this world and the next. Great, great the blessing in store for the king who gives his heart to his Lord.

In His two Tablets to Napoleon III, Bahá'u'lláh impresses on the Emperor the oneness of mankind whose many maladies will not be cured unless the nations, abandoning the pursuit of their several interests, agree together and unite in common obedience to the plan of God. The human race should be as one body and one soul. A far higher degree of faith than the world has ever reached before is demanded by God of every man in this Era. All are commanded to teach the truth and to work for God's cause: but no one will produce good results in this service unless he first purify and ennoble his own character.

Bahá'u'lláh bids the clergy give up their seclusion, mingle in the life of the people and marry. God is calling men to Him in this Age, and any theology which takes its own theses as a standard of truth and turns away from Him is deprived of value and efficacy.

He has come to regenerate and unite all mankind in very deed and truth and He will gather them at the one table of His bounty. Let the Emperor call on His name and declare His truth to the people.

Grave warnings and open or implicit threats if the kings do not acknowledge the Manifestation and obey His commands are contained in all these Tablets, especially in this to Napoleon III. The collective Tablet addressed to all the kings is, however, stern and minatory beyond the rest. Bahá'u'lláh warns the rulers that if they do not treat the poor amongst them as a trust from God; if they do not observe the strictest justice; if they do not compose their differences, heal the dissensions that estrange them and reduce their armaments, and follow the other counsels now given them by the Prophet, "*Divine chastisement shall assail you from every direction and the sentence of His justice shall be pronounced against you. On that day ye shall have no power to resist Him and shall recognise your own impotence. Have mercy on yourselves and on those beneath you.*"

Christ long centuries before had wept over the city whose children had ignored His visitation and refused His protection. Now at His second coming the same event recurred. But they who brought down the wrath of God on themselves were not the members of a nation but of an entire world.

Before He passed away Bahá'u'lláh proclaimed: "*The hour is approaching when the most great convulsion will have appeared.*" And again, "*The time for the destruction of the world and its people hath arrived.*"

More than forty years after the dispatch of these Tablets 'Abdu'l-Bahá, the son of the Prophet and the appointed Exemplar of His Faith, being freed at last from prison by the Young Turks, made a three years' tour of Europe and America. Saddened by many things He saw, and knowing the doom to which the heedlessness of the nations was hurrying them, He was sparing of denunciation, reproach or criticism; instead, with words of cheer and undiscriminating love He summoned His hearers to high, heroic action. He spoke much of the spiritual and social goal set by God for this enlightened Age : "*The Most Great Peace.*" He Himself in His joy, in His serenity, in His love for all, in His wisdom, His strength and resolution and utter submissiveness to God, seemed the incarnation of the Spirit of that Peace. His very presence brought receptive souls into touch with a state of being of which they might have heard but which none of them had ever known. Through many months of missionary work He explained the moral and spiritual conditions which would make possible the

Most Great Peace, and developed in many addresses the practical means by which it could be approached. In the United States, at Wilmette on the shores of Lake Michigan, He laid the foundation stone of the first Bahá'í Temple of the West, round which are to be grouped buildings devoted to social, humanitarian, educational and scientific purposes, the whole to be dedicated as one scheme to the glory of God and the service of man. He also saw in America the first beginnings of the building of the Administrative Order of Bahá'u'lláh.

But the general response of the public was not sufficient to stem the tides flowing towards war. Before He left the United States, 'Abdu'l-Bahá foretold the outbreak of hostilities in two years' time.

When at last peace was made, He declared that the League of Nations as constituted could not prevent war; and before He passed away in 1921 He announced to His followers the outbreak of another war fiercer than the last.

To many, at the opening of the second Bahá'í century, mankind seems to be drifting in a helmless barque upon a stormy and uncharted sea. But to the Bahá'í's another vision is revealed. The barriers by which men blocked their path to progress are torn down. Human pride is abased, human wisdom stultified. The anarchy of nationalism and the insufficiency of secularism are thoroughly exposed.

Slowly the veil lifts from the future. Along whatever road thoughtful men look out they see before them some guiding truth, some leading principle, which Bahá'u'lláh gave long ago and which men rejected. The sum and essence of the best hopes of the best minds to-day is garnered in such a simple statement as that of 'Abdu'l-Bahá's "Twelve Points":

1. Unfettered search after truth.
2. The oneness of mankind.
3. Religion a cause of love and harmony.
4. Religion hand in hand with science.
5. Universal peace.
6. An international language.
7. Education for all.
8. Equal opportunities for both sexes.

9. Justice for all.
10. Work for all.
11. Abolition of extremes of poverty and wealth.
12. The Holy Spirit to be the prime motive power in life.

The immense, complex, baffling task of unifying all peoples is set forth in its complete and inmost simplicity by 'Abdu'l-Bahá in seven pregnant phrases:

1. Unity in the political realm.
2. Unity of thought in world undertakings.
3. Unity of freedom.
4. Unity in religion.
5. Unity of nations.
6. Unity of races.
7. Unity of language.

Already the Bahá'ís have begun in deed and in fact to build the instrument destined to be the model and the nucleus of the Most Great Peace. The Administrative Order is as simple as it is profoundly conceived, and it can only be conducted by those whose lives are animated by love and fear of God. It is a system in which such opposites as unity and universality, the practical and the spiritual, the rights of the individual and the rights of society, are perfectly balanced not through arranging a compromise but through the revelation of an inner harmony. Those who have the experience of operating the Order testify that it seems to them like a human body which is made to express the soul within.

On the lake shore at Wilmette stands the completed Temple of Praise, a sign of the Spirit of the Most Great Peace and of the Splendour of God that has come down to dwell among men. The walls of the Temple are transparent, made of an open tracery cut as in sculptured stone, and lined with glass. All imaginable symbols of light are woven together into the pattern, the lights of the sun and the moon and the constellations, the lights of the spiritual heavens unfolded by the great Revealers of to-day and yesterday, the Cross in various forms, the Crescent and the nine pointed Star (emblem of the Bahá'í Faith). No darkness invades the Temple at any time; by day it is lighted by the sun whose rays flood in from every side through the exquisitely perforated walls, and by night it is artificially illuminated and its ornamented shape is etched with light against the dark. From whatever side the visitor approaches, the aspiring form of the Temple appears as the spirit of adoration; and seen from the air above it has the likeness of a Nine-Pointed Star come down from heaven to find its resting place on the earth.

But for the leading of the peoples into the Promised Land, for the spiritualising of mankind, for the attainment of the Most Great Peace the world awaits the arising of those whom the King of Kings has summoned to the task—the Christians and the Churches of the West.

"Verily Christ said 'Come that I may make you fishers of men' and to-day We say 'Come, that We may make you quickeners of the world' . . . Lo ! This is the Day of Grace ! Come ye that I may make you kings of the realm of My Kingdom. If ye obey Me you will see that which We have promised you, and I will make you the friends of My Soul in the realm of My Greatness and the Companions of My Beauty in the heaven of My Might for ever."

NABÍL'S HISTORY OF THE BÁB

HERE ONCE AGAIN in human history is the Light shining in a darkness that comprehendeth it not! Here once again is Faith re-arisen upon the world, bringing a New Day, shedding a new glory, calling men from sleep to a new life.

Here once again is Religion that men had thought sunk for ever in impotence—religion in its freshness, its purity and its power, religion reborn with all the magic of that ancient sweetness and beauty with which it was clothed in Holy Writ of old—religion warming men's hearts with a new compassion and loving-kindness, melting all estrangements, uniting many wills in a common devotion, a common sympathy, giving to life a new completeness, transcending sorrow and pain and death!

We of the western world may be unable to trace in human affairs about us the providence of God, may not see His path opening before our feet, may not be aware of His activity and presence in our midst, we may be divided one against another, may be full of fears, devoid of love, laden with deepening doubt.

But here are men and women, boys and girls who through faith reborn became possessed of a knowledge to which we are strangers, entered into an experience which we hardly believe to exist, whose eyes were opened to the Light from heaven, who had ears to hear the voice of God, and being changed from their old selves, transformed into new creatures, translated to a new degree of life, were by divine grace endowed with a courage, an energy, a blissfulness which has no likeness on the earth and which no earthly privation can impair.

They had none of these things through which we of the West give expression to our religion: they had no systems of theology and ethics, no traditions, dogmas, creeds, institutions. Love and obedience and joy (love for God and His prophet, the joy of obeying the divine summons, even to the extent of sacrificing for love's sake all they had and all they were)—these and these only were the marks of their religion.

All we have heard or read of the birth of a World Religion among men—of the Advent of a Divine Teacher, of the simple beginnings of His work, of the charm of His personality, of the love that He awakens in His followers, of His courage and authority, and His ability to overcome the whole world by the lonely power of His word—all this is here again; and the facts and the details and the circumstances of His coming are transcribed into the pages of this chronicle. He calls on men to leave the idols and the torpors of the past, to awake and to greet the Dayspring from on High; to join the legions of light and partake with him in the approaching world-triumph of God. Thousands upon thousands flocked to His banner, young and old, high and low, learned and unlearned, men and women, boys and girls. Thrilled with a new-born faith, animated with a magical love they acclaimed His prophethood and without reserve offered themselves as criers of the New Advent, torch-bearers of the New Revelation. When the envy of the mosque and the court stirred up far and wide against them the latent fire of Muslim fanaticism, they found in the strain that was put upon them a means of showing forth before men what power of soul God gives in their extremity to those who love Him utterly before all else.

With eager courage they challenged every form of persecution—ostracism, impoverishment, privation, beating, torture. Transported with a divine hope, sustained by an unshakeable resolution they counted suffering for God's sake a supreme blessing, and measured the greatness of their spiritual privilege by the anguish of their bodily pain. They welcomed martyrdom and endured its cruellest pangs with a serenity that moved their executioners to wonder and that bore immortal witness to the truth of the Faith for which they died. They knew no fear, no doubt; weariness could not relax their resolution, nor cloud their confidence.

Throughout the entire length of the action of this narrative, in the darkest hour of tragedy and of defeat, there sounds the call of assured victory, of triumph and of celestial joy. No human circumstance, however desperate, can chill or depress the ardour of the faithful. No physical privation, no hunger, no pain, no bereavement, no sorrow nor the violent hand of death can blot from their vision the sweetness of the Beloved's face or weaken the heart-beats of their impassioned adoration.

Here is no disquisition on the nature of Faith, no analysis of its elements. Here rather is Faith itself, Faith put to the proof, Faith in action, Faith naked, unarmed, alone, standing at bay against a thousand foes and remaining ever serene, unwavering, indomitable. Here is trust in God which impels not only the old but the young, to cast away their pleasures, their hopes, their careers, the joys of friendships and of home since thereby they can the better serve the will of Him Whom they love better than all mortal things. Eager, earnest, ardent, they find in the sacrifice they offer to their Beloved a sweeter, dearer happiness than otherwise is within the reach of created man.

Here once more is the Messenger of God, God's image mirrored in an all-perfect Love, God's power poured forth among men stirring them to a new spirituality, opening to them new reaches of consciousness. Here in very deed and in a form and fashion that none can gainsay or disown, is the vindication of the reality of religion, the proof of its present power in this modern world. Here is the re-affirmation of the dignity of human nature and of the infinite greatness of the purpose of human life.

Not in the dream of a saint, nor the vision of a seer nor the imagination of a poet is this given, but in the prose of a chronicler who sets forth in detail the course of actual historical events in a contemporary record that bears its own mark of truthfulness and is corroborated by extraneous evidence from a hundred sources.

The author, known to history as Nabíl, was himself a believer, a Persian, a follower of the Báb and afterwards of Him for Whose advent the Báb made ready the way. From the summer of 1849, at the time of the siege of Fort Tabarsí, he shared as an avowed believer in the dangers and adventures of his companions, and escaping with his life, he accumulated memories and made friendships which were to serve him well later in the compilation of material for this work. In the course of his narrative,* he tells

---

*The Dawnbreakers: Nabíl's Narrative of the Early Days of the Bahá'í Revelation, translated by Shoghi Effendi. Bahá'í Publishing Trust, Wilmette, Illinois

how as a boy, while he tended his master's sheep upon the
Persian hills, he would dream of a religion more real than that in
which he had been brought up and of a spirituality more pure
than that of the ecclesiastics who were his appointed teachers.

When in the summer of 1847, at the age of fifteen, he heard of
the Revelation of the Báb, he felt intuitively, at once, that here his
dreams had come true and he had of a surety found the religion
for which in the lonely thoughts of his heart he had so eagerly
longed.

He made inquiries, he pursued his investigations, he pondered
over what he learned, he felt that contagion of felicity which
marked the Bábís; and after two years, convinced of the truth of
the Báb's Prophethood, he openly espoused the Faith and spent
the rest of his life in the hazards and vicissitudes of its service.

He was possessed of a vigorous and ready pen; and his ardour
and constancy as a believer brought him the best of opportunities
for composing such a recital of the deeds of the Bábí pioneers as
this. No detached observer or scholar, however inquisitive or
industrious, could be in so favourable a position as this trusted
Bábí for collecting detailed and intimate information concerning
the early believers and their doings. He stood close to the heart
and centre of the Movement; he presented it with sympathy and
understanding, and he gave his work a vividly dramatic quality by
reflecting so clearly the spiritual experience of his heroes and by
reproducing with power their feelings, their motives and their
aspirations. He shared their enthusiasm and their high purpose in
full measure; and his narration is sustained throughout by that
profound impassioned love which gave to the crusade in those
days its rushing irresistible force.

How wonderful the intuition that could reveal to him a truth
utterly hidden from the learning and the culture of the great world
in his day! How wonderful the steadfastness that could preserve
him in his faith through a thousand adversities and sustain him
through the long toils of preparing this invaluable compilation.
He has his reward. This love-inspired tribute to the heroes he
honoured before all on earth stands an immortal monument to his
own illustrious memory, and in after ages will draw to him an

unfailing stream of grateful thoughts from the believers of many generations.

The volume of Nabíl's work now published in an English rendering recites the activities of the Báb during His ministry and pursues the fortunes of his followers for two years after His martyrdom. It covers a period of some eight years, and closes with the final expulsion of the Faith from the land of its origin. The narrative is intensely human, vivid, realistic. It presents a panorama of the entire movement in a series of pictures, incidents, episodes, some sketched in brief, some expanded in much detail, but all set forth in a style clear, graphic, powerful, glowing with the radiant fire of the author's unfailing enthusiasm.

The date chosen by the Báb for making known His status as a World Prophet and for inaugurating His Ministry was May 23rd, 1844. The declaration was made in His house in Shíráz to Mullá Husayn, who became the first of His Apostles, or His "Letters of the Living Word," with the particular designation of the "Bábu'l-Báb," or the Gate of the Gate.

The full account which Mullá Husayn gave of this momentous interview to Mírzá Ahmad-i-Qazvíní, the martyr, has been preserved by Nabíl, and it contains the following description of the immediate impression made by the Báb upon the first believer:

"This Revelation, so suddenly and impetuously thrust upon me, came as a thunderbolt which for a time seemed to have benumbed my faculties. I was blinded by its dazzling splendour and overwhelmed by its crushing force. Excitement, joy, awe and wonder stirred the depths of my soul. Predominant among these emotions was a sense of gladness and strength which seemed to have transfigured me. How feeble and impotent, how dejected and timid I had felt previously! Then I could neither write nor walk, so tremulous were my hands and feet. Now, however, the knowledge of His Revelation had galvanised my being. I felt possessed of such courage and power that were the world, all its peoples and its potentates to rise against me, I would, alone and undaunted, withstand their onslaught. The universe seemed but a handful of dust in my grasp. I seemed to be the Voice of Gabriel personified, calling unto all mankind:

" 'Awake, for lo! the morning Light has broken. Arise, for His Cause is made manifest. The portal of His grace is open wide; enter therein, O peoples of the world! For He, who is your promised One, is come!' "

The call of Mullá Husayn was the opening of the Báb's campaign.

As mysteriously Mullá Husayn had been drawn into the presence of the Báb, so the other disciples came to Him, spontaneously and of their own accord, within a few days of His Declaration. After brief instruction, He sent them out far and wide to bear His Message to various parts of the land. Each was to send back to Him the names of all the converts who definitely identified themselves with the New Faith: these the Báb would classify and record.

To Husayn He gave a special mission; and as soon as He was assured of its success, He set forth on October 10th, 1844, with Quddús, the greatest of all the believers, on the distant and difficult mission He had reserved for Himself. He struck at the strategic centre of the Muhammadan Faith, and went on the pilgrimage to Mecca and to Medina, to reveal the Cause of God in those sacred spots and to rekindle there, in the spiritual heart of Islám, the Ancient Fire which had so completely disappeared from among men.

He chose, as the recipients of His Message, two individuals whom He knew to be spiritually capable of appreciating it: Mírzá Muhít-i-Kirmání and the Sherif of Mecca. Both were men of distinction and influence. If they had the courage to follow the leading of their intuitions and to accept the Revelation, others would follow and the progress of the Cause would be rapid and wide.

Unfortunately for themselves and for their country, neither one nor the other of them proved willing to answer the divine summons. One evaded it, the other ignored it.

Bitterly disappointed, the Báb returned in June, 1845, to

Persia. Already in many parts of the land the tidings of the New Faith had been spread by these eager apostles, and had been warmly welcomed by the people. Sundry officers of church and state were quick to suspect that this movement boded them no good and they took alarm from the first. When the Báb went to Shíráz and began there to propagate His Cause with immediate and marvellous success, the Governor of the Province, moved with envy, ordered his arrest, cast him into prison, and determined on his death. The Báb, however, was finally released and permitted to go to Isfáhán. Here again He instantly won the hearts of the people. Thousands resorted to him to hear His Message. The priests were stung by jealousy and seventy of them in solemn conclave condemned Him to death for heresy. A friend, however, the Mu'tamidu'd-Dawlih, had interested Muhammad Sháh in the Báb's Revelation, and by the Sháh's order the Báb was taken under escort to interview his Majesty in Tihrán. Shortly before He reached the capital, He received from the Sháh a letter, written under the influence of the Grand Vizier Hájí Mírzá Áqásí, in which the promised interview was indefinitely postponed, and the Báb was relegated to a lonely fortress in the wild mountains of northern Persia.

Now a deepening darkness rapidly gathered round the fading fortunes of the Prophet. After nine months' incarceration in Máhkú where His personality, as by magic, won over the people of the neighbourhood, His jailers, and the warden of the castle, He was transferred by His enemies, in April, 1848, to a still more rigorous imprisonment in Chihríq.

At the same time, the persecution of the Bábís throughout the country was intensified and attacks upon their persons and their property grew more general and more violent. In October of that year, a number of believers in Mázindarán seeking refuge from their assailants withdrew to a disused fort, where they stood at bay for months before their enemies, who were supported by the regular army of the Sháh. In May, 1849, being promised that persecution would cease, they gave themselves up and were at once seized and done to death by their perfidious foes. Nine of the Báb's apostles, including Mullá Husayn and Quddús, with numbers of other distinguished Bábís, perished in this massacre.

In March of the following year occurred the death of the Seven Martyrs of Tihrán, an episode which has become notorious on account of the prominence of the sufferers, their high character and the publicity of their execution.

Two months later, in Nayríz, a large party of Bábís retreating before their tormentors were surrounded by their enemies and after a stout resistance were destroyed, in circumstances like those of their fellow-believers in Mázindarán. Their leader was Siyyid Yahyáy-i-Darabí, known as Vahíd, one of the principal dignitaries of the Persian church, and the most learned of all the Báb's followers.

At the same time in Zanján, a similar investment of Bábí refugees occurred, but on a much larger scale. As many as seventeen regiments of the regular army, together with artillery, were employed on this occasion against the Bábís who were led by another brilliant divine of Islám, known among the Bábís as Hujjat.

The Grand Vizier of the Sháh,* who had become the arch enemy of the Cause, now concluded that the spirit of the Bábís could not be broken nor the reform movement quelled so long as its Author remained alive. He determined therefore to put the Báb Himself to death. Dispensing with the formalities of any legal process, he, by use of the weight of his official position, had the Báb removed from Chihríq to Tabríz and there summarily condemned to death without trial.

The sentence was carried out in the public square of the city, on July 9th, 1850. A curious circumstance delayed for a few minutes the actual execution. The Báb, with a follower who was to die with Him, was suspended by a rope to a wall, and the firing squad of 750 rifles delivered a volley at close range. The heavy smoke obscured completely the wall and those who hung upon it. When it cleared away, the two condemned men were found to have escaped injury. The rope which bound them had been cut, and the Báb's companion was seen to be standing on the ground unhurt. The Báb had disappeared and was discovered in His prison, whither He had returned to finish a conversation which

* The Amír-Nizám, Mírza Taqí Khán.

had been interrupted when his jailors came to lead Him out to execution.

The members of the firing party, terror-stricken at such a prodigy, refused to lift their rifles again against the person of the Prophet, and the authorities were obliged to summon another regiment to consummate their crime.

The news of their Lord's martyrdom soon reached the Bábís standing at bay in Zanján. They were stunned and horrified but not disheartened. Outnumbered, they held out to the last limit of their strength; and when by force and guile their resistance at last was crushed, hundreds of Bábís, men, women and children passed through the red gates of martyrdom to the Great Beyond, and then rejoined their beloved Master, who had travelled by the same road so short a time before.

By the early autumn of 1850, the reactionaries had, as it seemed, cowed the main body of the believers and had destroyed every Bábí that had shown any capacity for leadership, except two only: Bahá'u'lláh who had espoused the Cause from the first, and Táhirih, the one woman-member of the nineteen apostles.

Through the efforts of these two, and especially the activity of Bahá'u'lláh, the Faith continued to make headway, until in August, 1852, an attack by a deranged Bábí on the person of the Sháh gave the authorities a pretext for a general slaughter of believers throughout the country, with the express aim of exterminating the Faith. Táhirih was martyred. Bahá'u'lláh with His dependents was exiled for life.

At this point, when all was at its darkest, and when to all except a few illumined spirits the light of the Cause of God seemed to be quenched for ever, the first volume of Nabíl's Narrative closes.

Faith in God and in His Prophet is the great ideal of the entire action—the sure touchstone to distinguish good from evil, truth from untruth. Righteousness is extolled by the Báb and the highest standard of conduct demanded by Him of His followers, but the purpose of Nabíl was no more to deal in the principles and practice of ethics than to set forth a new theological system.

His purpose was to show how Faith had come back into the world and had transformed those in whose hearts its flame was kindled. If his story is epic in the elevation and sublimity of its subject matter, it is in its mood lyrical—a lyric of Faith and of the love that Faith awakes. In the central foreground stands the figure of the Báb. No space is given to sketching the historical, the social or political background. There is almost no setting to the incidents, the minimum of description, no account of the general circumstances of the time. All the figures in the story, and they are to be counted by hundreds, are grouped around the Báb. Those who choose to turn towards Him are seen irradiated by the glory of their Lord; the intenser their Faith the more brilliant the light in which they are bathed. Those who turn away from Him lie in the horror of a darkness which deepens with the gradations of their unbelief. If Nabíl did not set himself to write a formally ordered history he produced a work which has the vital and informing unity that belong to a composition having a single hero, a single theme and one all-pervading dominant emotion. Everywhere in his book Nabíl sets forth Faith as the first of virtues, the first step of man upon the highroad to the presence of God.

Deploring the failure of one of Shaykh Ahmad's disciples to recognise the real dignity of a Prophet of God, he comments:

"His faith was weighed in the balance, and was found wanting, inasmuch as he failed to recognise that He Who must needs be made manifest is endowed with that sovereign power which no man dare question. His is the right 'to command whatsoever He willeth and to decree that which He pleaseth.' Whoever hesitates, whoever, though it be for the twinkling of an eye or less, questions His authority, is deprived of His grace and is accounted of the fallen."

Mullá Husayn himself, the Gate of the Gate, hardly showed the requisite measure of submissiveness. He proposed to apply a test by which He would put the Báb to the proof. "Had you not been my guest," said the Báb to him afterwards, "your position would indeed have been a grievous one. The all-encompassing grace of God has saved you. It is for God to test His servants and not for

His servants to judge Him in accordance with their deficient standards."

He told the first of his apostles whom He sent out: "Your faith must be as immovable as the rock, must weather every storm and survive every calamity . . ."

In his address to the others He said: "The very members of your body must bear witness to the loftiness of your purpose, the integrity of your life, the reality of your faith, and the exalted character of your devotion . . . Heed not your weaknesses and frailty; fix your gaze upon the invincible power of the Lord, your God, the Almighty . . . Arise in His Name, put your trust wholly in Him, and be assured of ultimate victory."

The apostles of the Báb spontaneously through the vigour of their own intuition recognised and adhered to Him. He Himself when in Mecca standing within the most sacred shrine of Islám approached the famous divine Mírzá Muhít-í-Kirmání, and put his faith to the test with a definite categorical demand . . . "Verily I declare," He said, "none besides Me in this day whether in the East or in the West can claim to be the Gate that leads men to the knowledge of God: My proof is none other than that proof whereby the truth of the prophet Muhammad was established. Ask Me whatsoever you please: now at this very moment I pledge Myself to reveal such verses as can demonstrate the truth of My mission. You must choose either to submit yourself unreservedly to My Cause or to repudiate it entirely. You have no other alternative. If you choose to reject My message, I will not let go your hand until you pledge your word to declare publicly your repudiation of the truth which I have proclaimed. Thus shall He who speaks the truth be made known, and he that speaks falsely shall be condemned to eternal misery and shame. Then shall the Way of Truth be revealed and made manifest to all men."

The great churchman was broadminded enough to perceive the truth of the Báb's pronouncement; else the Báb would not have approached him in that manner. He did not dare to deny it. But neither on the other hand did he dare to face the consequences of the public admission which the Báb demanded. He procrastinated. He pretended acceptance and promised submission;

then broke his word and fled. "I shall never depart from Medina," he assured the Báb, "whatever may betide, until I have fulfilled my covenant with You." As the mote which is driven before the gale he, unable to withstand the sweeping majesty of the Revelation proclaimed by the Báb, fled in terror from before His face. He tarried awhile in Medina and, faithless to his pledge and disregardful of the admonitions of his conscience, left for Karbilá.

Some years later the Muhít, still tormented in conscience, attempted to approach Bahá'u'lláh, the Báb being dead.

"Tell him," was Bahá'u'lláh's reply, "that in the days of My retirement in the mountains of Sulaymáníyyih, I in a certain ode which I composed set forth the essential requirements from every wayfarer who treads the path of search in his quest of truth. Share with him this verse from that ode: 'If thine aim be to cherish thy life, approach not our court, but if sacrifice be thy heart's desire, come and let others come with thee. For such is the way of faith, if in thy heart thou seekest reunion with Bahá; shouldst thou refuse to tread this path, why trouble us? Begone!' If he be willing, he will openly and unreservedly hasten to meet Me; if not, I refuse to see him."

Once again, the Muhít's courage failed. He refused to face the consequences of a confession of faith, withdrew and died an unbeliever.

In prison, on the night before His martyrdom, the Báb subjected his three devoted companions to a test of the most extreme severity. He was in a strange elation of spirits. The sadness that for long had weighed him down on account of the death of so many of his followers had vanished. The joy of His approaching sacrifice, the sense of the certain triumph of God's Cause, had dissipated every sorrow. Turning to His disciples He expressed regret that He was to die at the hand of an enemy instead of the hand of a friend. "Would that one of you," He said, "might now arise and with his own hands end my life." They shrank at the thought of taking a life so dear, so precious. Then one of them sprang to his feet and said that whatever the Báb commanded he would do. His companions interposed; and the Báb because he had shown himself ready to obey to the uttermost, chose him to share on the morrow the crown of martyrdom with his Lord. On the next morning, at the place of execution, he was tied in such a position that his head reposed on the breast of the Báb, and by the violence of the fusillade the two bodies were "shattered and blended into one mass of mingled flesh and bone."

The New Revelation was oftentimes accepted not so much through intellectual submission to an argument as through the inspiration of a spiritual experience.

The Báb and His followers invited and welcomed scrutiny and careful examination of His teachings; lectures by Bábís were frequently given and the faithful were always ready to meet anyone in intellectual controversy. In some important cases (as in that of the illustrious Vahíd and of Nabíl himself) investigation played a great part in conversion. But logical conviction was always supported or anticipated by a strong intuitive impulse. In very many cases the divine illumination was seemingly perceived by the force of sheer insight.

In his account of the call of the Eighteen Apostles Nabíl writes:

"Each of the twelve companions of Mullá 'Alí in his turn and in his own unaided efforts, sought and found his Beloved. Some in sleep, others in waking, a few whilst in prayer, and still others in their moments of contemplation experienced the light of this Divine Revelation and were led to recognise the power of its glory."

The conversion of Ismu'lláhu'l-Asdaq, a distinguished Bábí of Isfáhán, through a vision of the Báb (an experience not unparalleled in this chronicle) is quoted in his own words.

Hearing Mullá Husayn had come to Isfáhán he sought him out and met him at night in the home of Mírzá Muhammad 'Alíy-i-Nahrí.

"I asked Mullá Husayn to divulge the name of Him who claimed to be the Promised Manifestation. He replied, 'To inquire about that name and to divulge it are alike forbidden.' 'Would it then be possible,' I asked, 'for me, even as the Letters of the Living, to seek independently the grace of the All Merciful and through prayer to discover His identity?' 'The Door of His grace,' he replied, 'is never closed before the face of him who seeks to find Him.' I immediately retired from his presence, and requested his host to allow me the privacy of a room in his house where alone and undisturbed I could commune with God. In the midst of my contemplation, I suddenly remembered the face of a Youth whom I had often observed while in Karbilá, standing in an attitude of prayer, with His face bathed in tears, at the entrance of the shrine of the Imám Husayn. That same countenance now reappeared before my eyes. In my vision I seemed to behold that same face, those same features, expressive of such joy as I could never describe. He smiled as He gazed at me. I went towards Him, ready to throw myself at His feet. I was bending towards the ground, when lo! that radiant figure vanished from before me. Overpowered with joy and gladness I ran out to meet Mullá Husayn who, with transport received me and assured me that I had at last attained the object of my desire."

Of the call of Quddús, the last and greatest of the apostles, he writes: "The next day in the evening hour as the Báb followed by Mullá Husayn was returning to His home there appeared a youth dishevelled and travel-stained . . . Fixing his gaze upon the Báb, he said to Mullá Husayn: 'Why seek you to hide Him from me? I can recognise Him by His gait. I confidently testify that none beside Him whether in the East or in the West can claim to be the Truth . . .' "

The narrative continues.

" 'Marvel not,' observed the Báb, 'at his strange behaviour. We have in the world of spirit been communing with that youth. We know him already. We indeed awaited his coming . . .' "

Of the inclusion of Táhirih, the one woman among the apostles, Nabíl records that ". . . we have seen how instinctively she had been led to discover the Revelation of the Báb and how spontaneously she had acknowledged its truth. Unwarned and uninvited, she perceived the dawning light of the promised Revelation breaking upon the city of Shíráz, and was prompted to pen her message and plead her fidelity to Him who was the Revealer of that Light."

The Message which the Bábís proclaimed was primarily one of faith. "Raise the cry," said the Báb to Mullá Husayn, as He sent him out on his first missionary journey; "Awake, awake! for lo! the Gate of God is open, and the morning Light is shedding its radiance upon all mankind. The Promised One is made manifest; prepare the way for Him, O people of the earth! Deprive not yourselves of its redeeming grace, nor close your eyes to its effulgent glory."

The appeal which the Message made was felt to be quite extraordinary and to partake of the nature of pentecostal fire. Nabíl expresses this very definitely in his account of the progress of the Bábí movement in the province of Khurásán.

"There blazed forth," he writes, "in the heart of Khurásán a flame of such consuming intensity that the most formidable obstacles standing in the way of the ultimate recognition of the cause melted away and vanished. That fire caused such a conflagration in the hearts of men that the effects of its quickening power were felt in the most outlying provinces of Persia."

Their hearts aflame with this divinely kindled fire, the Bábís feared no danger, were daunted by no terror, and yielded under no adversity. They endured without a murmur manifold sorrows and sufferings. Indeed they counted it a high and precious privilege to go through tribulation for their Faith's sake, and looked forward to persecution with joy.

"Ever since the beginning of this holy enterprise, upon which I have embarked," cried Mullá Husayn, "I have vowed to seal with my life blood my own destiny. For His sake I have welcomed immersion in an ocean of tribulation. I yearn not for the things of this world. I crave only the good pleasure of my beloved. Not until I shed my blood for His name will the fire that glows within me be quenched."

Those chiefly responsible for the attacks on the Bábís were the officials of the state-church who owed their privilege and power to the ignorance and superstition of the people and were quick to see that the onrush of this crusading reformation movement would sweep them and all their depravities away for ever unless it was instantly and remorselessly strangled. They used their influence to rouse their fanatical followers in the name of orthodoxy against the innovators. A supine and apathetic government made no effort to quell disorder or to prevent violence. On the contrary, the officials of the state were inclined not only to wink at but even to take part in the riots, the plunderings and the massacres. The Bábís had no protection, no redress, no assurance or hope of justice. Before them lay the clear prospect of ostracism, of spoliation and probably of torture and death.

As one of the Bábís who were driven to bay in Zanján stated in answer to the denunciations of the Amír-Túmán: "God knows that we are and will ever remain loyal and law-abiding subjects of our sovereign, with no other desire than to advance the true interests of his government and people.

"We have been grievously misrepresented by our ill-wishers. No one of the Sháh's representatives was inclined to protect or befriend us; no one was found to plead our cause before him. We repeatedly appealed to him, but he ignored our entreaty and was deaf to our call. Our enemies, emboldened by the indifference which characterised the attitude of the ruling authorities, assailed us from every side, plundered our property, violated the honour of our wives and daughters, and captured our children. Undefended by our government and encompassed by our foes we felt constrained to arise and defend our lives."

Nothing that the armies of corruption could do acted as a deterrent to the Bábís. Faith had quickened in their hearts so impetuous and unquenchable a flame of heavenly love that earthly danger and suffering held no terrors for them. As love prompted them, as their Master bade them, they went forward on their crusading way, proclaiming their belief, calling aloud the Glad Tidings, summoning all men to give heed and not to remain blind to the light of so glorious a Day. The foreknowledge of destruction heightened their enthusiasm and intensified their activity.

Vahíd from the day he gave his adhesion to the cause, yearned to lay down his life for his Lord's sake, and testified to his joy when before the siege of Nayríz he saw the longed-for day was approaching.

Mullá Husayn when he had raised the Black Standard, before the siege of Mázindarán commenced, knew what the issue would be, and warned his followers in time.

"I together with seventy-two of my beloved companions shall suffer death for the sake of the Well-Beloved. Whoso is unable to renounce the world, let him now at this very moment depart, for later on he will be unable to escape."

Hujjat shortly before his death, when he had just seen his own wife and child killed by the enemy, testified to his own premonitions of suffering for the Báb's sake and to his joy therein.

"The day whereon I found Thy beloved One, Oh my God," he cried, "and recognised in Him the Manifestation of Thine eternal Spirit, I foresaw the woes that I should suffer for thee. Great as have been until now my sorrows, they can never compare with the agonies that I would willingly suffer in Thy name. How can this miserable life of mine, the loss of my wife and of my child, and the sacrifice of the band of my kindred and companions, compare with the blessings which the recognition of Thy Manifestation has bestowed on me! Would that a myriad lives were mine, would that I possessed the riches of the whole earth and its glory, that I might resign them all freely and joyously in Thy path."

The Báb early in His ministry knew the fate that awaited Him at its end. On their return from the pilgrimage to Mecca, He said good-bye to His beloved companion Quddús and told him sadly that they would not see each other again on earth; that Quddús would soon meet a martyr's death. "But," He said, "on the shores of the Great Beyond, in the realm of immortality, the joy of an eternal Reunion awaits us . . . I, too, shall tread the path of sacrifice . . ."

Nor was this high, heroic spirit of devotion found only in the leaders, or in the men; it was displayed likewise by women, by girls, by children, by all.

Táhirih, that outstanding star of Persian womanhood, the one woman-apostle of the Báb, of whom Professor Browne said that if the Bábí cause had done nothing else, to have produced such a woman as her in such a time and such a country would have made it illustrious—Táhirih, beautiful, exquisite, learned, eloquent, showed a courage and enterprise in spite of the disability of her sex which made her conspicuous even among the Bábís; when her time of martyrdom drew near she met it with rapture and endured a painful death with dignity and calm.

Nabíl records how numbers of girls and boys and aged men in the siege of Tabarsí or Nayríz or Zanján played their full part with the other Bábís in the defence of the asylum to which they had been driven; how mothers would encourage their children to suffer and to die rather than repudiate their faith; how the protracted resistance of the Bábís at Zanján was due in no small measure to the activity of the Bábí women who ministered to the sick and wounded, repaired the barricades, sewed garments, baked bread, cheered the faint-hearted and restored the faith of the wavering, while even the children showed the same enthusiasm as their elders and did what their tender strength permitted to the good of the common cause; and when at length the defenders were overwhelmed, the women endured with steadfastness the cruelties heaped upon them till they found release from their tormentors in a martyr's death.

To the believer in the Báb and in Bahá'u'lláh this account of the Heroic Age of the Faith is precious and moving beyond words: it inspires, it stimulates, it fortifies.

But also to another class of readers (a class which at present, unfortunately for the world, is much larger) this work of Nabíl's has an extraordinary interest. It claims the particular regard and deserves the most patient study of every student of religious history and of everyone who believes in the reality of Divine Revelation. For here in Nabíl's work is a direct account of one of those august events which occur at rare intervals in the progress of humanity and which are fraught always with the most momentous consequences: the birth of a new World Religion.

As the Bábí Faith is distinguished from all earlier religions in this respect, that the knowledge of it spread almost instantly from the East to the West; so this record which Nabíl made of its beginnings, holds in the history of comparative religion a position in certain respects altogether unique.

The world (no doubt through its own fault) has to lament that there has been preserved so little authentic information as to the rise of the great Religions of ancient times, as to the life and death of their Founders, as to the efforts and heroisms and fate of their immediate followers. In nothing is the sad truth that the world knows nothing of its greatest men more unhappily conspicuous than in the meagreness of testimony concerning the Authors of the successive World Revelations of the past.

The eager interest and loving reverence of the faithful have in later years made so much of the little information that is available; deficiencies, too, have been so well filled in by tradition, by legend or even by myth; and enthusiastic scholars have so often assumed an air of certitude about matters which prove on scrutiny to be merely conjectural, that there is current a gravely exaggerated idea as to our real knowledge of the rise of any of the world religions prior to Islám.

The personality and the philosophy of Buddha seem to have charmed the western world more than that of any other non-Christian prophet. Generous tributes to the beauty and sweetness of his character and to the loftiness of his spiritual wisdom are to be found in the writings of many a Christian divine, and his teachings are accessible to the English public in a variety of popular editions.

Yet the immensity of Buddhistic literature serves only to set off the paucity of contemporary or early written records and does not remove the obscurity which hangs about the details of the Prophet's life or the origin of his teaching. The fact that some sceptical scholars have explained Buddha away as a sun-myth and have questioned the antiquity of the Buddhist tradition is of no great interest save as testifying to the uncertainty which subsists about the whole matter. One of the best known English authorities (Mrs. Rhys Davids, *Buddhism*, pp. 17-18) admits that the Pali Canon was not committed to writing till

80 B.C. (about one hundred and sixty years after the teaching had been introduced into Ceylon; and four hundred years after the death of Buddha himself). She concludes that the life of Buddha "as a historical fact, is at least as well demonstrated as that of the founder of any other religion" of antiquity and that the story of his life however "draped and embroidered with myth and legend" cannot be dismissed as historically untrue without "extravagant recourse to forced interpretations, and assumptions of improbable happenings. . . ."

The New Testament has been the guide and inspiration of western religion for nineteen centuries; but everybody must wish that extant accounts of the life and teaching of Jesus Christ were less brief and fragmentary, and those who cherish this wish most warmly are those who love Him best and seek to discern and follow His way most earnestly. Of the early teachers of Christianity, the confessors and martyrs of the first three centuries of our Era, we know much less than about the Founder Himself. Many volumes were in those days written with fine art and preserved with zealous care concerning the history of Rome, the conquests of Caesar and the like; but the history of the Christian Faith was looked on as a wholly inconsiderable matter. The cultivated world of that period had not the least conception of the relative importance of the New Revelation. They did not trouble to make any note of its development nor in those unruly and indiscriminating times did they regard such records as the Christians themselves made to be of sufficient interest to be preserved.

The meagreness of the information we possess about the age of the Christian martyrs is lamented by the learned and conservative Mosheim. He writes: "The actions and sayings of those holy martyrs from the moment of their imprisonment to their last gasp were carefully recorded in order to be read on certain days and thus proposed as models to future ages. But few, however, of these ancient acts are come down to our times . . . From the eighth century downwards several Greek and Latin writers endeavoured to make up this loss by compiling with vast labour accounts of the lives and actions of the ancient martyrs. But most of them have given us little else than a series of fables adorned with a profusion of rhetorical flowers and striking images, as the wiser even among the Romish doctors frankly acknowledge. Nor are these records that pass under the name of martyrology worthy of superior credit since they bear the most evident marks both of ignorance and falsehood. So that upon the whole this part of ecclesiastical history for want of ancient and authentic monuments is extremely imperfect and necessarily attended with much obscurity."

Gibbon remarks in the fifteenth chapter of his history: "the scanty and suspicious materials of ecclesiastical history seldom enable us to dispel the dark cloud that hangs over the first age of the church," and in a footnote to the sixteenth chapter: "In the various compilations of the Augustan history (a part of which was composed under the reign of Constantine) there are not six lines that relate to the Christians; nor has the diligence of Xiphilin discovered their name in the large history of Dion Cassius."

Naturally we know more about the great figures of early Islám than about those of other religions, for the Faith arose in more recent times, its extension was amazingly rapid, and it developed within a very few centuries a culture of a most brilliantly intellectual type. But our information concerning Muhammad's personality and His teaching, about His immediate companions and followers, seems to be scanty enough. It has not been sufficiently full or conclusive or authentic to prevent an extraordinary variety of interpretation and belief as to Muhammad's character and actions, and little of it has till very recently been accessible to western readers. Gibbon scandalously caricatured the Prophet, whom he called "an illiterate barbarian." The genius of Carlyle moved him in 1840 to protest that "our current hypotheses about Mahomet that he was a scheming impostor, a Falsehood Incarnate, that his religion is a mere mass of quackery and fatuity, begins really to be now untenable to anyone. The lies which well meaning zeal has heaped round this man are disgraceful to ourselves only." But this warning has been little heeded and western scholars may be found to describe Muhammad as "a brigand chief," and the like, even in this present century.

More than twelve centuries elapsed between the rise of Muhammad and the rise of the Báb whom He foretold; world-conditions in the interval changed and progressed, and anyone who investigates the Bábí religion is enabled to learn the true facts concerning the Founder and His immediate followers with a degree of fullness and accuracy never before possible in human history. No earlier Revelation is so well documented as this. It came to mankind at the same time as the railway, the telegraph, the telephone. How great the significance of the little casual fact that one of the very earliest English references to the Bábí Faith sets forth the execution of the Bábís in 1852 as given in the *Teheran Gazette* of that day!* The Báb's crusade was so vigorous, and it was shared in by so many eminent persons, that it attained the widest publicity in Persia and threatened to shake the whole corrupt ecclesiastical system. Though the country was backward and weak, yet Britain and Russia had there important imperial interests which brought many foreign residents, official and otherwise, to the capital. Some of these were sufficiently interested in the Movement to spread the knowledge of it in Europe. Western references to the Báb date back as far as 1851, and have been (some on a large and some on a small scale) continuous since that time. Some of the more important of these references are to be found in Comte de Gobineau's "Les Religions et les Philosophies dans l'Asie Centrale, ' and in Lord Curzon's "Persia and the Persian Question."

Professor Browne, of Cambridge University, gives the names of four Persian histories as adverting to the religion, one of them at great length, and has himself in such works as *A Traveller's Narrative* and *Materials for the Study of the Bábí Religion*, made public a large amount of early information on the progress of the Faith. Three volumes of the Báb's own works have been translated by A. L. M. Nicolas and published in France.

Amid the great and ever-growing library of works on the Báb,

*Lady Shiel's *Glimpses of Life and Manners in Persia*, 1856.

the Chronicle of Nabíl's holds a most conspicuous place. While
it is informal and unofficial; while it is not used by the Bahá'ís to
determine any point of teaching, yet it is as nearly as may be the
Bábís' own story of the Báb's crusade. It is not in a philosophic
sense a history: it is not an ordered exposition of the development
of the Báb's Revelation. Nabíl is as much an editor as an author.
He gathers items of information with care, industry and eager
zeal for truth, and pieces them together in their proper chrono-
logical sequence. For the most part he sets forth this or that event
as he had it from some believer who had taken part in it, or had
witnessed it, or had heard of it from an eyewitness. He enjoyed
in his labours the special help of some of the members of the
inmost circle of the Faith, including the brother of Bahá'u'lláh
and the amanuensis of the Báb. Bahá'u'lláh Himself saw a portion
of the manuscript of Nabíl and expressed His general approval
and acceptance of it. It has in the fullest degree the character of
a Bábí Gospel. If we possessed an authorised and large scale
account of the Acts of Jesus Christ written by one of the Twelve
and preserved in the form in which it came from the author's pen,
we would have a Christian Gospel as authentic in its sphere as this
of Nabíl's in its. Here with a distinctness and in a detail un-
equalled in any early literature of the world we can examine the
manner in which a Great Revelation comes among men and can
study the phenomena of a dawning Age of Faith before any
system of theology or of organisation has taken shape and when
the Prophet shows forth His majesty through the exertion of a
quickening spiritual power which awakes in the true-hearted an
altogether miraculous enthusiasm and courage and at the same
time stirs the obscurantists and the vicious to deeds of hate and
fear and cruelty.

In this respect, the value of Nabíl's work is enhanced by the
fact that its composition is itself one of the products of the
Prophet's creative power. The spirit which impels the pen of
Nabíl is the spirit of the other Bábís. His mental attitude as an
author is the same as that of the heroes who form his subject.
Faith in the Báb as the Prophet of God prompted him to under-
take this work. Faith sustained him to its completion. Faith

invigorates every sentence and word in it. As one reads one is conscious that the outlook, the mood, the style of the book reflect the same eager, buoyant, irresistible faith as inspires the lofty exploits it records. By a thousand proofs Nabíl shows his desire to be fair and just to all; but at the same time he writes as an avowed and eager and determined participant in a life and death struggle in which neither side gives nor expects quarter, but which must be fought out to an end. The temper of the writing resembles that of a battle song in which (even in moments of what seem irredeemable defeat) the note of assured triumph transcends all other notes.

The future will be better able than we to set events in their true perspective, to appraise the value of the vast amount of historical material which the industry of Nabíl has amassed and to judge the significance of these deeds of heroism and self-sacrifice.

Yet there is one respect in which this work has a particular timeliness now, which it will not have in the future. We live and long have lived in a twilight age, and with deepening fear have watched the darkness close in upon us. Religion, organised or not, has more and more lost its control over men's conduct, its hold upon their hearts. Churchmen are as little able as statesmen to unravel the perplexities of the situation, to inspire hope for the future, to formulate a plan for staying the general disintegration and for reconstructing an adequate world order. Believers turn their sad thoughts back to the early days of the Christian Faith. They stretch their longing hands far across the intervening centuries to ancient Pentecosts—but in vain. They read in the Scriptures of the miracles of courage and achievement wrought by the power of divine faith in past ages. They turn to the Epistle to the Hebrews and light upon such a tribute to Faith as this:

"And what shall I more say? For the time would fail me to tell of Gideon, and of Barak, and of Samson, and of Jephthah; of David also, and Samuel, and of the prophets:

"Who through faith subdued kingdoms, wrought righteousness, obtained promises, stopped the mouths of lions.

"Quenched the violence of fire, escaped the edge of the sword, out of weakness were made strong, waxed valiant in fight, turned to flight the armies of the aliens.

"Women received their dead raised to life again: and others were tortured, not accepting deliverance; that they might obtain a better resurrection:

"And others had trial of cruel mockings and scourgings, yea moreover of bonds and imprisonment:

"They were stoned, they were sawn asunder, were tempted, were slain with the sword: they wandered about in sheepskins and goatskins; being destitute, afflicted, tormented;

"(Of whom the world was not worthy:) they wandered in deserts, and in mountains, and in dens and caves of the earth."
(Hebr. XI. v. 32-38.)

They wonder at the vision, the exultation, the prevailing power of the faithful ones of old who, though they were in their own time little noted and obscure, yet for all their apparent weakness could not be gainsaid but went forth in their Master's cause, removed mountains of doubt, uplifted the characters of men and of peoples, and amid the ruins of an unhappy and decaying world inspired and initiated the building of a new and greater civilisation. Christians to-day long bitterly, despairingly, for that ancient Glory. But the chasm seems unbridgeable. Between us and the comrades of the Christ a great gulf is fixed which none may cross. Understanding and creative power were theirs. To us belong bewilderment, frustration and despair.

THE THEME IS VICTORY

But to read Nabíl is to enter an utterly contrasted world. To peruse this chronicle of events not yet a century old, to feel the warm glow of love and faith and militant ardour with which the narration is suffused, to observe the character of the Báb, in which the sweetest charm and humility are mingled with majesty and power, is to pass suddenly into a realm of thought wholly different from that in which we of the West so long have lived. As we read, we realise we are following here the fortunes of people of our own time, whose outlook on life is exactly that which

Christians once had but now have lost, exactly that of which we read in our Scriptures and for which we repine in vain. Here, indeed, in this record is darkness—spiritual darkness such as now gathers in the West, darkness awful and immeasurable. But it lies only at the far circumference, at the outer edges of the scene, not at the heart of things. It is darkness challenged, darkness routed, scattered, put to flight and to eternal shame. The central place is held by light; the theme is the victory of light. The darkness serves to set off the light by contrast. It cannot reach nor touch the souls of the Bábís. In them there is no perplexity nor apprehension. Human pain and failure are for them overpassed and lost in a divine attainment. They did not trust human wisdom nor find as we have done that it betrayed them. They trusted God wholly and for love's sake gave up all they had and were, that they might serve His Truth.

Whatever is base, unworthy, ignoble in human nature is not here glorified, extolled, palliated, but held up to execration, destined to final defeat and complete destruction. Glory and praise and dominion and the certainty of triumph belong here to whatever in human nature is most lovable, most noble, most sublime.

Here are men, women and children, a vast, motley, heterogeneous host of young and old, learned and unlearned, the rich man and the poor man, the aristocrat and the labourer: gathered into one indissoluble body not by any outward compulsion or constraint whatever, but of their own free act and eager choice. The tie that binds them is spiritual only—simply love for God— and is so strong that no enticement or repulsion of the earth can break or loosen it. Neither prison nor poverty, hunger nor thirst nor wounds could force them to desert their comrades, deny their Lord or abandon His cause: severally, or in multitudes together, they would face and welcome death, and give their lives, as their Beloved Lord gave His, simply to serve the cause of God among men.

We need not go back to ancient Scriptures or to distant times, to the early history of the Christian Church, to the Epistles to the Hebrews or to the Old Testament, to rediscover that faith in God which in our extremity seems lost beyond recall. We need not imagine that the outpourings of God's manifest power, the open vision of His Beauty, the ecstasy of self-sacrifice in His cause, have passed away forever from the earth.

All these things are in our midst!

'ABDU'L-BAHÁ

A Study of a Christlike Character

"No one, so far as my observation reaches, has lived the perfect life like 'Abdu'l-Bahá."†

To live to-day in deed and truth the kind of life that Jesus of Nazareth led and bade His followers lead; to love God wholeheartedly, and for God's sake to love all mankind, even one's slanderers and enemies; to give consistently good for evil, blessings for curses, kindness for cruelty and, through a career darkened along its entire length by tragic misrepresentation and persecution, to preserve one's courage, one's sweetness and calm faith in God—to do all this and yet to play the man in a world of men, sharing at home and in business the common life of humanity, administering when occasion arose affairs large and small and handling complex situations with foresight and firmness—to live in such a manner throughout a long and arduous life, and when, in the fullness of time, death came, to leave to multitudes of mourners a sense of desolation and to be remembered and loved by them all as the servant of God—to how many men is such an achievement given as it has been given in this age of ours to 'Abdu'l-Bahá?

To the historian, the psychologist, the student of comparative religion, the narrative in all its aspects has much to offer of interest and value. But to the would-be Christian of the twentieth century the personal life and character of Sir Abbas Effendi (more widely known as 'Abdu'l-Bahá) make a direct and peculiar appeal.

An ordinary man who has set himself really to follow the precepts of Christ finds himself in special difficulties to-day. The very understanding and knowledge of the will of Christ, as well

---

†T. K. Cheyne, D. Litt., D.D. *The Reconciliation of Races and Religions.*

as the performance of it, seem now less easy to attain than they
were for our forefathers. The accuracy of the Gospel record not
only in phrase and detail, but in larger matters likewise is, however unjustifiably, questioned by a number of scholars. The
record in any case is brief and fragmentary; and the utterances
attributed to the Christ are not only very few but so terse and
epigrammatic that their bearing is often uncertain and they admit
of diverse interpretations. The problems of the contemporary
world, too, are so much more complex than those of the period
in which Christ lived that His words which suited so well the
conditions of the past are difficult to apply to the present. Those
who profess themselves the teachers of Christendom speak, as a
whole, with such different voices and offer such contradictory
advice that there is much bewilderment.

Guidance from both the ancient book and from living example
seems, therefore, to the man in the street less easy to gain than it
was once. And the natural weakness of our nature which finds so
arduous the moral life demanded by Christ is no longer supported
by custom and general opinion, but is, on the contrary, unhappily
enervated by the influence of a self-willed and flippant age.

In the story of 'Abdu'l-Bahá the Christian comes upon something which he ardently desires and which he finds it difficult to
obtain elsewhere. There awaits him here reassurance that the
moral precepts of Christ are to be accepted exactly and in their
entirety, that they can be lived out as fully under modern conditions as under any other, and that the highest spirituality is quite
compatible with sound commonsense and practical wisdom.
Many of the incidents in 'Abdu'l-Bahá's life form a practical
commentary on the teachings of Christ and dramatise the meaning
of the ancient words. Being a philosopher as well as a saint, He
was able to give to many a Christian enquirer explanations of the
Gospel-ideal which had the simple authority both of His con-
sistent life and of their own reasonableness.

Christ taught that the supreme human achievement is not any
particular deed nor even any particular condition of mind; but
a relation to God. To be completely filled—heart, mind, soul—
with love for God, such is the great ideal, the Great Command-

ment. In 'Abdu'l-Bahá's character the dominant element was spirituality. Whatever was good in His life He attributed not to any separate source of virtue in Himself but to the power and beneficence of God. His single aim was servitude to God. He rejoiced in being denuded of all earthly possessions and in being rich only in His love for God. He surrendered His freedom that He might become the bond-servant of God; and was able, at the close of His days, to declare that He had spent all His strength upon the Cause of God.

To Him God was the centre of all existence here on earth and heretofore and hereafter. All things were in their degree mirrors of the bounty of God and outpourings of His power. Truth was the word of God. Art was the worship of God. Life was nearness to God; death remoteness from Him. The knowledge of God was the purpose of human existence and the summit of human attainment. No learning nor education that did not lead towards this knowledge was worth pursuit. Beyond it there was no further glory, and short of it there was nothing that could be called success.

In 'Abdu'l-Bahá this love for God was the ground and cause of an equanimity which no circumstance could shake and of an inner happiness which no adversity affected and which (it is said) in His presence brought to the sad, the lonely or the doubting the most precious companionship and healing. He had many griefs but they were born of His sympathy and His devotion. He knew many sorrows, but they were all those of a lover. Warmly emotional as He was He felt keenly the troubles of others, even of persons whom He had not actually met or seen, and to His tender and responsive nature the loss of friends and the bereavements of which He had to face more than a few brought acute anguish. His heart was burdened always with the sense of humanity's orphanhood, and He would be so much distressed by any unkindness or discord among believers that His physical health would be affected. Yet He bore His own sufferings, however numerous and great, with unbroken strength. For forty years He endured in a Turkish prison rigours which would have killed most men in a twelvemonth. Through all this time He was, He said, supremely happy, being close to God and in constant communion with Him. He made light of all His afflictions. Once, when He was paraded through the streets in chains, the soldiers, who had become His friends, wished to cover up His fetters with the folds of His garments that the populace might not see and deride, but 'Abdu'l-Bahá shook off the covering and jangled aloud the bonds which He bore in the service of His Lord. When friends from foreign lands visited Him in prison, and seeing the cruelties to which He was subjected, commiserated with Him, He disclaimed their sympathy, demanded their felicitations and bade them become so firm in their love for God that they, too, could endure calamity with a radiant acquiescence. He was not really, He said, in prison: for *"there is no prison but the prison of self,"* and since God's love filled His heart He was all the time in heaven.

From this engrossing love for God came the austere simplicity which marked 'Abdu'l-Bahá's character. Christ's manner of life had been simple in the extreme. A poor man, poorly clad, often in His wanderings He had no drink but the running stream, no bed but the earth, no lamp but the stars. His teaching was given in homely phrases and familiar images, and the religion He revealed, however difficult to follow, was as plain and open as His life. His very simplicity helped to mislead His contemporaries. They could recognise the badges of greatness but not greatness itself, and they could not see light though they knew its name. He was neither Rabbi nor Shaykh, though He was the Messiah. He had neither throne nor sword, though all things in heaven and in earth were committed into His charge.

The life of 'Abdu'l-Bahá, too, was simple and severe. Familiar during much of His life with cold, hunger and all privation, He chose for Himself in His own home the most frugal fare. The room in which He slept (sometimes denying Himself even the comfort of a bed!) served Him as a workroom too. His clothing was often of the cheapest kind; and He taught His family so to dress that their apparel might be *"an example to the rich and an encouragement to the poor."* The household prayers which He held morning and evening were quite informal.

Partly from a natural modesty but also from a resolve to do

nothing that might encourage in others a tendency to formalism, He objected to any parade or unnecessary ceremonial, particularly if He were to be concerned in it.

Even if some degree of circumstance and formality were called for, He would reduce them to the smallest possible proportions. When, on April 17th, 1921, He was to receive from Lord Allenby in the grounds of the Governor's residence at Haifa the honour of knighthood for services rendered to the people of Palestine during the Turkish occupation, He evaded the equestrian procession and military reception prepared for Him, by slipping unobserved from His house and making His way to the rendezvous by some unaccustomed route. When all were in perplexity and many thought that He was lost He appeared quietly at the right place and at the right time and proceeded in the prescribed manner with the essential part of the ceremony.

Of all material things, as of food, clothing, shelter, He sought and desired for Himself the barest sufficiency. But asceticism was not part of His creed nor of His teaching. "*Others may sleep on soft pillows; mine must be a hard one,*" He said once in declining a kind friend's offer of some little comfort for His room. Men were to take what God had given them, and to enjoy the good things of nature; but with renunciation. Fasting was a symbol, and as such had high value, but in itself was no virtue: "*God has given you an appetite,*" He said; "*eat.*" Riches He thought no blessing; if they had been, Christ would have been rich. The poverty, however, which He inculcated was not impecuniousness but the heart's poverty of him who is so rich in love for God that he is destitute of all desire for aught else.

He was the most unassuming of men. He counted himself personally as less than others, put Himself below them and served them in every way He could find with unaffected humility. He used to entertain at His table visitors from far and near; but if the occasion were one of special importance He would rise and wait on His guests with His own hands—a practice He recommended to other hosts.

When His Father was alive and dwelt outside 'Akká among the mountains, 'Abdu'l-Bahá used frequently to visit Him, and though the way was long He habitually went on foot. His friends asked Him why He did not spare Himself so much time and effort and go on horseback. "*Over these mountains Jesus walked on foot*," He said, "*and who am I that I should ride where the Lord Christ walked?*"

But this humility did not come from any weakness. It was a proof of His strength and a cause of His spiritual power. Once when a child asked Him why all the rivers of the earth flowed into the ocean He said: "*Because it sets itself lower than them all and so draws them to itself.*" Pride repels; humility attracts. When commenting on Christ's direction to be as little children, He emphasised the fact that the virtues of children are due to weakness, and adults must learn to have these virtues through strength. A palsied arm cannot strike an angry blow; but the virtue of forbearance belongs to one who can, but will not. His humility was not due to any diffidence or other failing. Nor did it imply any self-abasement or self-depreciation. What it meant was the obliteration of the personal self. His separate ego had no existence at all save only as an instrument of expression for the higher self that was one with God.

Somebody who knew Him in the West remarked that He was always master of the situation, and amid the novel and alien surroundings of such cities as London, Chicago and New York He preserved His self-possession and His power. On one occasion in America, when He arrived at a house where He was to be a guest at luncheon, a coloured man called on Him just before the meal hour. Being known to the hostess the caller was admitted, but 'Abdu'l-Bahá observed that, according to the prevailing social custom, there was no intention of admitting him to sit at the table with the regular guests. Now race-prejudice is what 'Abdu'l-Bahá could not tolerate: at His own table members of all races and religions met on an equality as brothers. He was not going to countenance it among His friends in America if He could help it. What was the surprise of the hostess and of everyone else present when He was observed clearing a place beside Him and calling for knives and forks for the new arrival. Before any seemly way of countering his initiative was found, before anyone had quite realised how it had happened, the lady found herself doing what neither she nor any other hostess in her position would have dreamed of doing, and entertaining at her table with her white friends a negro. 'Abdu'l-Bahá had become the spiritual host. He spread before those who sat with Him the sense of the common Fatherhood of God. Such was His radiant power that the unconventional challenging meal passed off without unpleasantness or embarrassment to any who partook of it.

When He was travelling in the West it was His custom to take out with Him a bag of silver pieces to give to the poor whom He met; and being brought down one evening to the Bowery Mission in New York He delivered there one of the most compassionate and moving of His addresses. It reads in part as follows:

"*To-night I am very happy for I have come here to meet my friends. I consider you my relatives, my companions, and I am your comrade. You must be thankful to God that you are poor, for His Holiness Jesus Christ has said: 'Blessed are the poor.' He never said 'Blessed are the rich.' He said, too, that the Kingdom is for the poor. Therefore you must be thankful to God that though in this world you are indigent yet the treasures of God are within your reach; and although in the material realm you are poor, yet in the Kingdom of God you are precious. His Holiness Jesus Himself was poor. He did not belong to the rich. He passed His time in the desert travelling among the poor, and lived upon the herbs of the field. He had no place to lay His head, no home; yet He chose this rather than riches. It was the poor who accepted Him first, not the rich. Therefore you are the disciples of Jesus; you are His comrades, your lives are similar to His life, your attitude is like unto His, you resemble Him more than the rich. Therefore we will thank God that we have been so blest with real riches and, in conclusion, I ask you to accept 'Abdu'l-Bahá as your servant.*"

At the end of the meeting 'Abdu'l-Bahá stood at the Bowery entrance to the Mission Hall shaking hands with from four to five hundred men and placing within each palm a piece of silver.

With no less tenderness He answered the need of those whose poverty was spiritual. His guards and jailers, servants of a cruel and despotic master, were won by His kindness and became His friends. "What is there about him," people would say, "that He makes His enemies His friends?"

Towards those who displayed to Him personal ill-will and malice He showed forbearance and generosity. Missionary work, He said, is not promoted by being overbearing and harsh; bad people are not to be won to God by criticisms and rebukes, nor by returning to them evil for evil. On the contrary, the Cause of God advances through courtesy and kindness, and the bad are conquered by intercession on their behalf and by sincere, unflagging love. "*When you meet a thought of hate overcome it with a stronger thought of love.*"

Christ's command to love one's enemies was not obeyed by assuming love nor by acting as though one loved them; for this would be hypocrisy. It was only obeyed when genuine love was felt. When asked how it was possible to love those who were hostile or personally repugnant, He said that love could be true yet indirect. One may love a flower not only for itself but for the sake of someone who sent it. One may love a house because of one who dwells in it. A letter coming from a friend may be precious though the envelope which held it was torn and soiled. So one may love sinners for the sake of the universal Father, and may show kindness to them as to children who need training, to sick persons who need medicine, to wanderers who need guidance. "*Treat the sinners, the tyrants, the bloodthirsty enemies as faithful friends and confidants,*" He would say. "*Consider not their deeds; consider only God.*" His kindness was persistent and unflagging; He forgave until seventy times seven. A neighbour of His in Haifa, a self-righteous Muslím from Afghanistan, who regarded 'Abdu'l-Bahá as an outcast, pursued Him for years with hate and scorn. When he met 'Abdu'l-Bahá on the street he would draw aside his robes that he might not be contaminated by touching a renegade. He received kindnesses with obdurate ill-will. Help in misfortune, food when he was hungry, medicine in sickness, the services of a physician, personal visits—all made no impression on his hardened heart. But 'Abdu'l-Bahá did not relax nor despair. For five and twenty years He returned continuously good for evil; and then suddenly the man's long hate broke down, his heart warmed, his spirit awoke, and with tears of disillusion and remorse he bowed in homage before the goodness that had mastered him.

Even with enemies much more dangerous and cruel than this poor Afghan, 'Abdu'l-Bahá showed the same forbearance and goodwill. He would suffer or invite any personal loss or humiliation rather than miss an opportunity of doing a kindness to an enemy; He would suffer calamity in order to avoid doing something which might be to the spiritual detriment of an ill-wisher. When 'Abdu'l-Bahá had been liberated, the misrepresentations of a secret enemy resulted in His re-imprisonment. He might probably have secured His release by a special appeal; but He declined to take this action. He went back to the prison and was held there for years, one reason for this non-resistance to evil being that the success of His appeal would but deepen the envy and degradation of His enemy: "*He must know that I will be the first to forgive him.*" In this submissiveness He acted in the same spirit as His Father in parallel circumstances. For during the period when a certain jealous member of their entourage was by various means covertly seeking His life, Bahá'u'lláh and all the members of His family, including His eldest son, remained (so Professor Cheyne records) on cordial relations with him, admitting him as before to their company, even though they thus afforded him further opportunities of pursuing his deadly designs.

So confident were all who knew 'Abdu'l-Bahá that they could count on his largeness of mind that even the Sháh of Persia, when in extremity and threatened with revolution, stooped to ask the advice of the man he had kept in prison for a lifetime, and received an assurance that if he would end despotism and establish a constitution he might count on a happy reign, but that if he persisted in his present path he would be dethroned. The Sháh neglected the counsel and brought down upon himself the fate from which his generous prisoner would have shielded him.

From his foot one may reconstruct Hercules, and from a few words and incidents one may reconstruct a character. 'Abdu'l-Bahá was no churchman; yet His qualities clarify the Christian ideal of manhood and help to prove for those who need such proof, how that ideal applies to modern as truly as to ancient conditions of life and is no less within the reach of active men to-day than it was in simpler times gone by.

QUEEN MARIE OF RUMANIA AND THE BAHÁ'Í FAITH

MONG THE BAHÁ'Í treasures in the International Bahá'í
Archives at Haifa there lies an exquisite and precious
brooch, preserved as a memorial of the first of the queens
of the world who recognised and acknowledged the
Revelation of Bahá'u'lláh.

Queen Marie of Rumania did not hesitate about this recognition
nor was she diffident about giving it expression. She was at the
time in bitter need, in profound, overwhelming sorrow. The
sweetness, the tenderness, the depth of sympathy and helpfulness
which she found at once in boundless measure in the Divine
Message made an instantaneous appeal and opened her heart to
seek and welcome the knowledge of its manifold beauty and
truth. She felt the precious, warm loving-kindness of the Heavenly
Teachers, the perfection of their understanding. Her soul was
satisfied. Here at last was that for which she had hungered. Here
was peace, the reality of peace: a breath upon a fevered world
from that guarded inner shrine where peace has its inviolate home.

She was in bitter need. Those who were near and dear to her
surrounded her with love and sympathy and consolations; for
they too knew grief and pain and felt with one who suffered so
acutely as she. But anguish of spirit had awakened in her a desire
for something other than the sincerest human condolence. She
faced the mystery of death and love. No word, no touch, however
gentle, that came only from a knowledge of this fleeting human
life could suffice her now. Loneliness had broken the hold of
earth on her. She longed, as she had never longed before, for God.

And God came.

Jesus Christ divided those to whom the Divine Message is
communicated into four classes: those who are too self-absorbed
to receive any impression, those who are able to receive only a
shallow impression, and those who are deeply impressed by the
truth but are also impressed by things not true, and finally those

who are single-minded in the love and service of truth. It was the unique distinction of Queen Marie that, living in a special sphere where the cares of this world and the deceitfulness of riches are at their maximum, she accepted and held fast to the New Revelation. She was the first to walk in that narrow path in which, when it is made broader, all the kings and queens and rulers of the earth will follow her.

The time of an Advent is and ever has been an epoch of the severest test for humanity. "Who may abide the day of His coming?" cried the ancient prophet; "and who shall stand when He appeareth?" For none is the test so hard as for the great and rich.

"*Know ye in truth,*" said Bahá'u'lláh, "*that wealth is a mighty barrier between the seeker and his desire, the lover and his beloved. The rich, but for a few, shall in no wise attain the court of His presence nor enter the city of content and resignation.*" For none among the great and rich is the test so hard as for royalty. Alone among those of royal blood, alone among her sister-queens, Marie of Rumania recognised the dawning of the Day of Days and acclaimed in Bahá'u'lláh the glory of the Father. Therefore this signal privilege has been accorded her; and the ornament which she presented as a sign of gratitude to the Bahá'í teacher who brought her the Divine Message is honoured with a place among the holy relics of the early heroes of the Cause who first upheld among man the Banner of the Manifest King of Kings.

Marie, the eldest daughter of the Duke of Edinburgh, was born in the purple; but she had this special distinction that in her veins ran the blood of the only two royalties to whom Bahá'u'lláh, when He announced His Advent to the world's rulers, addressed words of commendation. She was on her mother's side the granddaughter of Czar Alexander II, who abolished serfdom, and on her father's side of Queen Victoria; both of whom Bahá'u'lláh addressed in words different from the stern or minatory terms used by Him towards the King of Prussia, the Emperors of Austria and France, and the Sultán of Turkey and the Sháh of Persia.

She was herself an outstanding and radiant personality, vigorous and daring, devoted to idealistic and humanitarian projects. A traveller who in 1909, before her accession to the throne, visited her summer home in Sinaia, Rumania, at a time when it was unoccupied by her, wrote afterwards in *The Bahá'í Magazine*:

"We were deeply impressed with the spiritual atmosphere of her living apartment furnished largely with her own handiwork, the carving of the furniture, the paintings, the beautiful altar, all made by herself and all indicative of a deeply spiritual nature. Her books, her thoughts, as one gleaned in a hasty passage through her home, were such as to indicate the kind and spiritual ruler she has become."

After her death, an old friend who had known her since they played as girls together in Malta in 1888 wrote of her as follows:

"No one who ever had the privilege of personal or intimate acquaintance with Queen Marie could fail to be impressed by the greatness of her mind and spirit. Her own life story reveals so well her ardent and joyous nature, the depth of feeling that accompanied every thought and action . . . The world is the poorer for the passing of such a noble lady, and a blank, impossible to fill, is left in the lives of those who knew her personally. She had passed through and suffered so much, even her wonderful health was too sorely tried and we must be thankful in spite of the great loss to us all that she is at rest and spared any further suffering. Her spirit is surely near us still and we must try to follow her noble example of great endurance and courage to face whatever may await us in these troublous times."

—(Lilian McNeill, *World Order*, IV, 384).

The first tidings of the Bahá'í Teaching were brought to her in the early days of 1926 when her Majesty was in Bucharest and owing to personal sorrow was living in retirement. Martha Root, the best known of the pioneers of the Faith of Bahá'u'lláh, sent her a short note with a copy of Dr. Esslemont's *Bahá'u'lláh and the New Era*. The Queen accepted the book and was at once so keenly interested by its message that she sat up over it into the small hours, and the next morning she sent an invitation to Martha to visit her in the Palace on the following day at twelve o'clock.

So quick and strong was the impression made through that interview that the Queen gave it utterance that same year in many ways; public as well as private. She found a ready response to her enthusiasm in the young daughter Ileana, afterwards Archduchess Anton, to whom she taught these truths. She wrote to an American friend of hers in Paris, "I have found . . . all my yearnings for real religion satisfied . . . I am now ready to die any day full of hope; but I pray God not to take me away yet for I still have a lot of work to do." (*Bahá'í World*, VI, 580).

In May and in September, 1926, *The Toronto Daily Star* published from her pen two glowing tributes to the Bahá'í Faith. "It is a wondrous Message," she wrote, "that Bahá'u'lláh and His son 'Abdu'l-Bahá have given us. They have not set it up aggressively, knowing that the germ of eternal truth which lies at its core cannot but take root and spread . . . I commend it to you all. If ever the name of Bahá'u'lláh or 'Abdu'l-Bahá comes to your attention, do not put Their writings from you. Search out Their books and let Their glorious peacebringing, love-creating words and lessons sink into your hearts as they have into mine."

To *The Philadelphia Evening Bulletin* in September the same year she contributed an article on the Faith in the course of which she testified expressly to her acceptance of the truth of a succession of Revelations, a succession of Prophets—"Christ, Muhammad, Bahá'u'lláh," she wrote; continuing, "those voices (of God) sent to us had to become flesh so that with our earthly ears we should be able to hear and understand . . ."

These three articles being syndicated were printed in nearly two hundred American newspapers, and afterwards appeared in several newspapers in the East.

The Guardian of the Bahá'í Cause gratefully acknowledged these spontaneous appreciations. "Moved by an irresistible impulse," he wrote in the *Bahá'í World* for 1926-8, I "addressed to her Majesty in the name of the Bahá'ís of both East and West a written expression of our joyous admiration and gratitude for the queenly tribute which her Majesty has paid to the beauty and nobility of the Bahá'í Teachings . . ."

c

The following is the letter which he received in reply:

Bran, August 27th, 1926.

Dear Sir,

I was deeply moved on reception of your letter.

Indeed a great light came to me with the message of Bahá'u'lláh and 'Abdu'l-Bahá. It came as all great messages come at an hour of dire grief and inner conflict and distress, so the seed sank deeply.

My youngest daughter finds also great strength and comfort in the teachings of the beloved masters.

We pass on the message from mouth to mouth and all those we give it to see a light suddenly lighting before them and much that was obscure and perplexing becomes simple, luminous and full of hope as never before.

That my open letter was balm to those suffering for the cause is indeed a great happiness to me, and I take it as a sign that God accepted my humble tribute.

The occasion given me to be able to express myself publicly was also His Work—for indeed it was a chain of circumstances of which each link led me unwittingly one step further, till suddenly all was clear before my eyes and I understood why it had been.

Thus does He lead us finally to our ultimate destiny.

Some of those of my caste wonder at and disapprove my courage to step forward pronouncing words not habitual for Crowned Heads to pronounce; but I advance by an inner urge I cannot resist.

With bowed head I recognise that I, too, am but an instrument in greater Hands, and rejoice in the knowledge.

Little by little the veil is lifting, grief tore it in two. And grief was also a step leading me ever nearer truth, therefore do I not cry out against grief!

May you and those beneath your guidance be blessed and upheld by the sacred strength of those gone before you.

Marie.

Martha Root also wrote to her Majesty, and in the reply which she received were these words: ". . . The beautiful truth of Bahá'u'lláh is with me always, a help and an inspiration. What I wrote was because my heart overflowed with gratitude for the revelation you brought me. I am happy if you think I helped. I thought it might bring truth nearer because my words are read by so many . . ."

In the following year (1927) her Majesty gave another audience to Martha Root; a third audience in 1928 when with her daughter the Princess Ileana she was the guest of the Queen of Yugoslavia in Belgrade; and a fourth in 1929 in the Summer Palace at Balcic. She contributed an encomium of the Cause, charged with warm feeling and beautifully expressed, to the fourth volume of *Bahá'í World*; and another more brief but not less significant to the fifth volume. "The Bahá'í teaching," she wrote, "brings peace to the soul and hope to the heart. To those in search of assurance the words of the Father are as a fountain in the desert after long wandering."

It had been for some time her Majesty's wish and aspiration to visit in person the sacred shrines upon Mount Carmel and to meet in person Shoghi Effendi. In the year 1931 the opportunity, as it seemed, arrived. Accompanied by her youngest daughter her Majesty travelled to the Holy Land and arrived at Haifa with the intention of fulfilling her cherished desire. But fate had ruled otherwise. Unfriendly influences intervened. She did not reach her goal. In a sad letter to Martha Root dated June 28th, 1931, she told of her frustration and of the unwelcome pressure to which she had been subjected.

"Both Ileana and I," she wrote, "were cruelly disappointed at having been prevented going to the holy shrines and meeting Shoghi Effendi; but at that time we were going through a cruel crisis and every movement I made was being turned against me and being politically exploited in an unkind way. It caused me a good deal of suffering and curtailed my liberty most unkindly . . . But the beauty of truth remains and I cling to it through all the vicissitudes of a life become rather sad."

Early in 1934 her Majesty again received Martha Root in audience in the Controceni Palace in Bucharest and expressed her delight that the Rumanian translation of Bahá'u'lláh and The New Era had just been published in Bucharest and that her people were to have the blessing of reading this precious Teaching. In the course of the interview the Queen told of an incident which had happened in Hamburg some months earlier when she was en route to Iceland. As she was driving down the street a girl tossed into the car a little note, and when her Majesty opened it she read the message, "I am so glad to see you in Hamburg because you are a Bahá'í."

Martha Root's sixth and final interview took place in February, 1936 in the same Palace, and was in some respects the most touching and significant of all. Her Majesty spoke of various Bahá'í books, for she used to purchase them as they came off the press. She spoke of the depth of the *Iqán*, and of the wonderful radiant force of *Gleanings from the Writings of Bahá'u'lláh*. "Even doubters," she said, "would find a powerful strength in it if they could read it alone and would give their souls time to expand." She told how in London she had met a Bahá'í, Lady Blomfield, who had shown her the message that Bahá'u'lláh had sent to her grandmother, Queen Victoria. She told, too, of a dear friend of her girlhood who lived in 'Akká, Palestine, and knew Shoghi Effendi and had sent from there pictures of 'Akká and Haifa. This friend (Mrs. McNeill) published afterwards a letter which the Queen wrote to her at this time:

"Dear 'little' Lilian," it began, "it was indeed nice to hear from you and to think that you are of all things living near Haifa and are, as I am, a follower of the Bahá'í Teachings. It interests me that you are living in that special house; the Teachers so loved flowers, and being English, I can imagine what a lovely garden you have made in that Eastern climate. I was so intensely interested and studied each photo intently. It must be a lovely place and those south-eastern landscapes and gardens attract me with a sort of homesickness ever since our Malta days. And the house you live in, so incredibly attractive and made precious by its associations with the Man we all venerate . . ."

Four days after this, the Queen sent for *The Bahá'í World*, her last public tribute to the Faith of Bahá'u'lláh. It was in due course reproduced in facsimile as a frontispiece to Volume VI, 1936-38, and runs as follows:

"More than ever to-day when the world is facing such a crisis of bewilderment and unrest, must we stand firm in Faith seeking that which binds together instead of tearing asunder. To those searching for light, the Bahá'í Teachings offer a star which will lead them to deeper understanding, to assurance, peace and goodwill with all men.—Marie, 1936."

The end was drawing near. Her health undermined by her many troubles began to fail. After some months of illness, in July, 1938, she passed away, and leaving this world where for all her royal rank she had known so much of grief and tears she entered that Great Beyond of which she had thought so often and so deeply.

Her death and obsequies were attended with all the ceremonial that befits the passing of a Queen. But who can tell what was the greeting that awaited her on the other side where she learned in an instant how true had been her intuitions of the Manifestation of God and where she saw unobscured now by any mortal veil the white eternal splendour of the Truth that she, alone among the earth's queens, had risen to acclaim.

The Guardian of the Cause and the Bahá'ís generally recognised the distinction of her spiritual station and the greatness of her service to the Cause. In July, 1938, the Guardian on behalf of all the Bahá'ís sent a message of condolence to her daughter the Queen of Yugoslavia to which her Majesty replied expressing "sincere thanks to all Bahá'í followers." To the Memorial Service held in the Cathedral of Washington, D.C., U.S.A., the Bahá'ís of the United States and Canada sent a tribute of flowers. The following sentences are from an account of that ceremony:

"On July 25th, 1939, the first anniversary of the death of Queen Marie of Rumania, an impressive memorial service was held in her honour at the Cathedral of Washington in the national capital of the United States. In Bethlehem Chapel on this midsummer afternoon national dignitaries and humble citizens paid loving tribute to a royal personage whose name stands out with an especial lustre in the history of her time. The spiritual beauty of the service expressed the character of this noble Queen—the first member of royalty to embrace the Faith of Bahá'u'lláh.

"Arranged by the Rumanian Minister, Radu Irimescu, the service was conducted by the Reverend Doctor Anson Phelps

Stokes, canon of the Cathedral and former Secretary of Yale University. Among the diplomatists present were the British, French and Italian Ambassadors and representatives of other European embassies and legations. The Secretary of State, Honourable Cordell Hull, headed the American delegation which included government officials and representatives of the Army and Navy . . .

"Directly opposite the altar in this intimate chapel stood the imposing floral tribute 'from the Bahá'í Friends of America'—a cross ten feet in height with a nine-pointed star at its centre. This emblem was designed by Charles Mason Remey and presented in consultation with the National Spiritual Assembly. It was beside the Bahá'í tribute that the Rumanian Minister stood at the conclusion of the service to greet the audience as they passed out, according to the Continental custom on such occasions.

"Not only did Queen Marie as the Dowager Queen of Rumania attest her faith in the Divine Cause through private letters; she claimed the spiritual bounty of calling the Teachings to the attention of others."

In these dark and troublous times, this Day (or is it not rather this Night?) of Judgment, when there is no open vision and when the gift of spirituality is not esteemed, the connection of Queen Marie with the Bahá'í Faith may seem to be but a small matter, the least episode among the multifarious activities of a crowded and brilliant life. But when this sleep in which the world's soul is shrouded ends at last; when men's spirits awakening behold the glories and the bounties and the opportunities that have lain about them, unwelcome and unregarded, all these many years, then they will look back upon the past with a new and horrified understanding. They will gaze with amazement and indignation and pity upon the incorrigible blindness of the mighty ones of Europe who, despite the manifold warnings of God, led their people through misery upon misery and flung them at last into the ultimate abyss of war. But amidst that universal darkness of failure and misrule that fills the palaces and chancelleries of the world men will see one solitary light shining in lone splendour and will acknowledge the true majesty of that one reedeming soul whose high faith caught and reflected far the glory of the breaking Dawn of God.

In later times, when the prophecies of the Bible are fulfilled openly before the eyes of all, when the New Jerusalem is established in the top of the mountains and "the nations of them that are saved walk in its light and the kings of the earth bring their glory and honour into it"; then men will see treasured among the sacred relics of the first champions of the Bahá'í Faith one royal ornament, a brooch of silver and diamond, the memorial of the first Queen who recognised and acclaimed the Glory of Bahá'u'lláh; and the name and the deed of Queen Marie of Rumania will be on the lips of men forever.

THE CALL TO GOD

A MEDITATION

WHEN GOD CAME back into a world which had forgotten Him He sent as His herald His Best Beloved, the Báb, in whom the Spirit of Love was manifest with such radiance that His disciples knew him as "the Ravisher of Hearts." Bahá'u'lláh Himself in that little volume, *The Hidden Words*, into which He has distilled the essence of all revelations, teaches that before the foundation of the world God knew His love for man and therefore created him. He breathed within man "a breath of His own spirit"; "engraved on him His image," and bestowed on him endless bounties. One of these gifts, Justice, is "the sign of my loving kindness" since through its observance every man can win knowledge for himself.

The first demand which Justice makes on man is that he shall love his Creator. "I loved thy creation, hence I created thee. Wherefore, do thou love Me that I may name thy name and fill thy soul with the spirit of life . . . Love me, that I may love thee. If thou lovest Me not, My love can in no wise reach thee . . . My claim on thee is great: it cannot be forgotten." (H.W.A. 4, 5, 20.) Reunion with God is man's heavenly home. The love of God in man's Paradise. It is his stronghold, in which, if he enter in, he shall be safe and secure—But if he turn away therefrom he "shall surely stray and perish." (H.W.A. 9.)

Righteousness has two supports—both spiritual. One is the love of God—"Walk in My statutes *for love of Me*." (H.W.A. 38.) The other is the fear of God, without the restraint of which and the knowledge of the certainty of retribution, the selfishness of man could not be held in control. "We have admonished Our loved ones," writes Bahá'u'lláh, "to fear God, a fear which is the fountain head of all goodly deeds and virtues . . . The fear of God . . . is the chief cause of the protection of mankind, and the supreme instrument for its preservation." (Wolf. pp. 135 and 27.)

'Abdu'l-Bahá frequently adverted to the close relationship between faith and morality. For instance He wrote (Tablets, 549) "By faith is meant first, conscious knowledge and second, the practise of good deeds . . . Although a person of good deeds is acceptable at the threshold of the Almighty, yet it is first to know and then to do." (Tablets, p. 549.) "The cause of eternal glory to man," He writes, "is faith and certainty and then acting according to the behests of . . . the Eternal God." (Tablets 667.) God requires good deeds from one who loves Him. "Neglect not My commandments if thou lovest My beauty . . ." (H.W.A. 39.)

Through Faith and Righteousness, we are taught (and not without them) the world may be united. For the virtues are the means by which people are enabled to live together in peace and happiness. Generally speaking, whatever tends to harmony is right, and whatever promotes discord is wrong. Integrity, loyalty, fidelity, kindness, forbearance, mercy, generosity, trustworthiness, equity, hospitality, and the like, all tend to social concord, well-being and unity. If the scope and field of the virtues be not walled in by prejudices or bigotry, but expand without hindrance, then they will find their natural goal in uniting all the peoples of the globe. Faith will attract the help of the Holy Spirit without which the division forces of earth life cannot be mastered; and faith and the knowledge of God will alone be able to end that fierce struggle for existence which 'Abdu'l-Bahá calls "the fountain head of all calamities and the supreme affliction."

For Faith is a "divine elixir" which "transmutes the soul." When a believer turns in faith towards God a profound change in his being is wrought through which he becomes a "new creature." 'Abdu'l-Bahá likens this change to the ante-natal process whereby spiritual forces surrounding the body of an infant as it is formed before birth gradually permeate it according to the degree of its receptivity. Similarly a believer's faith draws about him the everlasting bounties of God which he by degrees appropriates into his being according to the measure of his capacity and of the spiritual preparation he has made. (Tablets 157.) Man's natural condition is that of an animal: until he is born again from this and detached from the world of nature he remains essentially an animal, "and it is the teachings of God which convert this animal into a human soul." (Letter to the Hague.)

The soul is an intermediary between the spiritual world and the material world. In its higher aspect it looks up toward the Kingdom of Glory, in its other aspect it looks downward toward the lower sphere where darkness and ignorance have their home. If spiritual light be poured down upon this lower phase of the soul and if the soul be able to receive it then the truth is made clear and falsehood is of short duration. But if such light does not come or is not accepted, then darkness gathers about the soul from all directions, it is cut off from the spiritual world and remains in the lowest depths. (Tablets p. 611.)

'Abdu'l-Bahá used the picture of the "Waxing of the Moon" to illustrate the gradualness of this heavenward conversion and detachment from the world. The believer when first he turns to God and receives his light is like the crescent moon which is illumined on its sunward side but has the face it turns to earth still in shadow. When the moon is full, and, turning to the sun's light the same face it turns to earth, is illumined throughout its whole circumference so that no shadow anywhere remains, it becomes a type of the spiritually mature soul. (Tablets 108.) The reality of this severance is shown by a remark attributed to 'Abdu'l-Bahá—"The Holy Spirit moves my limbs."

The results of spirituality, the full meaning of reunion with God, are not, however, made known to man fully till the Hereafter. "Sorrow not if, in these days and on this earthly plane, things contrary to your wishes have been ordained and manifested by God, for days of blissful joy, of heavenly delight are assuredly in store for you. Worlds, holy and spiritually glorious, will be unveiled to your eyes." (GI.329.)

The purpose of earth life is to acquire the qualities that will be needed in those other worlds: as "the knowledge and the love of God; faith, sanctity, spirituality, eternal life."

To a "pure, kind, radiant heart" is promised "a sovereignty ancient, imperishable and everlasting." Could man behold that immortal sovereignty, he would "strive to pass from this fleeting world." (H.W.P. 41.)

But the journey to God is not easy to accomplish. God is a jealous God. "Ye shall be hindered from loving Me and souls shall be perturbed as they make mention of Me. For minds cannot grasp Me nor hearts contain Me." Man must face a conflict in his own soul: "If thou lovest Me, *turn away from thyself;* and if thou seekest My pleasure *regard not thine own* . . . There is no peace for thee *save by renouncing thyself* and turning unto Me." (H.W.A. 7, 8.)

Only through the energy of his own volition may the hidden powers of his being be developed. Again and again man is called on "to make an effort." He is reminded that the greater his *endeavour* to cleanse and refine the mirror of his heart, the more faithful will be the reflection in it of the glory of the names and attributes of God, and that as a result of the exertion of his own spiritual faculties he will be able to "attain the courts of everlasting fellowship." (G.262.)

At the present time the way to God is particularly hard to find. For it is the Day of Judgment. Mankind has been "taken unawares," as Christ foretold it would be. God can only be known through His Messenger; and now there is a New Era, a New Advent, a New Messenger. Old forms and names do not avail now. Souls are being tested by their readiness to acknowledge the New Manifestation of God—as the Mosaists were tested by the advent of Christ. Men are being divided by God: some are taken, others left. All behold the light; only the spiritual see its source. All men recognise a transition; only the spiritual understand its meaning.

But no soul, no Age is tested beyond its powers. To those who seek to turn to God inspiration adequate to every demand is given. Great as have been the bounties poured forth from heaven in past Advents, those of to-day are greater far. Both in the Gospel and the Apocalypse the overwhelming weight of this Second Coming and the victory of the righteous over the infidel have been foretold. A power above the ken of men and angels, we are assured, now enforces men's obedience to the will of God.

The teachings on the spiritual life are such as beseem the age of man's maturity, when every soul is required to investigate the truth for himself. They are given in plain terms, not in "proverbs." They are authentic, being the written word of Bahá'u'lláh or 'Abdu'l-Bahá. They are not of doubtful interpretation. They are voluminous and comprehensive, offering diverse approaches to knowledge and being adapted to diverse temperaments. Owing to the labour of various translators and predominantly to that of the Guardian, many of these teachings are accessible in English.

The earliest and perhaps (it is said) the greatest of Bahá'u'lláh's revelations on the Search for God is a little mystical treatise: "The Seven Valleys." The thought is subtle and profound; the idiom is oriental; but yet the book has a beauty, a charm and a rapture which have made it the dearest treasure of many a believer. It is the love-story of one who being separated from his beloved seeks far and long, eagerly, patiently, despite all hardships and through all vicissitudes for the one and only object of his desire; and at last attains his goal in a union which will know no separation or end—"When a true friend and lover meets the beloved one, the radiance of the beauty of the beloved creates a fire which burns away all veils, burns all he has and all he is, consumes his very being, so that nothing remains but the friend."

The story is one of a journey. But though we read of 'valleys,' 'cities,' 'heights,' 'fields,' 'gardens,' yet it is made clear the changes of scenery are inward changes of emotion, of sensibility and the like. The traveller passes from ignorance to knowledge, from illusion to discernment; love deepens, is cleansed, intensified, uplifted; wisdom yields to greater wisdom; joy trembles and is lost to make way for finer joy. The "Seven Valleys" are seven experiences or groups of experiences which all must pass through who would travel this way to the end.

The story is lyric rather than dramatic. Though it is (like Bunyan's masterpiece) an allegory of a pilgrimage to a Celestial City, there are no lions, nor giants in the way here, no Doubting Castle, no Vanity Fair. The enemies of the traveller dwell within his heart. Evil is a negation, an imperfection. Nor is the journey lonely: the Beloved's presence is felt from the beginning, the Messenger of Love is the pilgrim's guide throughout: The moving impulse of the journey is not solely the traveller's own; the voice of his Beloved calls ever in his heart "seek thou no shelter save in the Bower of the Well-Beloved," and he is drawn onwards to the happy ending by a power not his own.

How far away these valleys from the earth we know to-day! How far these aims, this search from the pursuits and projects of men and peoples now. Yet we are given to understand that only by adopting "The Hidden Words" as the standard of right living and "The Seven Valleys" as a guide to human conduct will society be empowered to inaugurate the Most Great Peace.

The Obligatory Prayers are given to help a Believer in this search. They are not concerned with the objects so familiar at this time—as the expansion of the cause, the giving of the message, the unifying and pacification of the peoples. No. They are designed to be used daily by Bahá'í of all degrees for generations and centuries to come. They are about that which Bahá'u'lláh wishes to be the essence and constant centre of Bahá'í devotion and thought. Comprehensive and complex they may be: but their subject is one and simple. It is the knowledge and the love of God.

The Short Prayer states the whole matter in a word: "Thou hast created me to know Thee and adore Thee."

The Medium Prayer is more particular. It specifies in two verses the fact of the Manifestation. The first verse presents this in its transcendent aspect, proclaiming God's Advent and His Sovereignty. The second acknowledges His omnipresence and unity, gives the substance of His Revelation and remembers the champions of the Faith.

The Long Prayer develops the theme still more fully and deeply. It seeks the vision of God's Beauty, an approach to His presence, an eternity of progress in His knowledge. The main phases of the thought seem to be Self-Surrender, Confirmation, Adoration and Thanksgiving, Penitence, and Trust in forgiveness and redemption through the special graces of this Dispensation. While this Long Prayer has one definite, elevated subject, believers have found that they can apply it, or major parts of it, to a special crisis or a special act in their own lives and can thus the better understand the Prayer and spiritualise their problems.

How marked and how significant, on the one side the correspondence and on the other the contrast that exist between this prayer of the New Age and the Lord's Prayer which Christians have been repeating for nineteen centuries. Here is reflected the continuity of the work of Christ and Bahá'u'lláh and the Oneness of their common purpose. Here, too (in an hour when many fear Christ has thrown away His teaching on an unworthy race), is a testimony to the ultimate success of His glorious ministry and sacrifice.

The first petitions of the Lord's Prayer are for the coming of the Kingdom of God on earth.

The Obligatory Prayers imply and declare that the Kingdom has come: for instance "the All-Possessing is come. Earth and heaven, glory and dominion are God's . . ." and "He who hath been manifested is the Hidden Mystery . . . through whom the letters 'B' and 'E' have been joined and knit together . . ." (that is, mankind's true existence begins in the New Era).

The Lord's Prayer remembers a prophecy and a promise; and centres men's attention on a triumphant future on earth. The Obligatory Prayers contain no prophecy and aim at an inward spiritual attainment.

Christ's Prayer is social in form. It is suited to spiritual children, being very simple and largely practical. In the words "as we forgive those who trespass against us" it adverts to the virtue of personal mercy to which Christ gave special prominence.

The Prayer of Bahá'u'lláh is personal and mystical, advanced in character and suited to a maturer race. It carries the idea of communion and unity far, invoking in the Long Prayer all the Prophets of the Ages, interceding for the past heroes of the Faith, and joining the worshipper's testimony to this Era and its Prophet with the testimony of those in the highest heaven and of the Tongue of Grandeur itself as well as with that of all creation.

Besides these and similar prayers, the Guardian has given us in the volume Prayers and Meditations a number of other prayers of a different origin—prayers made by Bahá'u'lláh for His own use, acts of communion between the Prophet Himself and the Most High.

To these a special mystery attaches, as He Himself affirms (p. 282), and they are bequeathed to us by His particular grace. They offer us a new approach to the knowledge of God, and constitute perhaps the highest point we can attain in our mystical contemplation of the Prophet's ministry.

Some of these pieces are ascriptions to the power, the exaltation and the munificence of God. Others deal with His creative and redemptive work. Others belong to dramatic moments in His struggle against the evil forces of His environment. The range of thought and emotion which we find in them far outreaches ordinary human experience. On the one hand it soars to un-imagined heights of adoration and triumph and joy. On the other, it plumbs depths of such anguish as only the truest love could know. But whatever the subject or the occasion of these prayers they all are one continuing diverse song of self-surrender and praise and thanksgiving to God. From every page—now in phrase or in sentence or paragraph or sometimes in a whole long prayer of glowing and sustained emotion—pour forth tributes of adoration magnifying the eternal Beauty of Him whose love gives sustenance to the universe and who with one least drop from the infinite ocean of his Mercy now redeems and beatifies mankind.

Love for God inspires every thought and deed. "In Thy path and to attain Thy pleasure, I have scorned rest, joy, delight. . . . I have wakened every morning to the light of Thy praise and Thy remembrance, and reached every evening inhaling the fragrances of Thy mercy . . . The fire of Thy love that burneth continually within me hath so inflamed me that whosoever among Thy creatures approacheth me and inclineth his inner ear towards me cannot fail to hear its raging within each of my veins." (pp. 103, 270). "Nothing whatsoever can withhold me from remembering Thee, though all the tribulations of earth were to assault me from every direction. All the limbs and members of my body proclaim their readiness to be torn asunder in Thy path and for the sake of Thy pleasure, and they yearn to be scattered in the dust before

Thee. O, would that they who serve Thee could taste what I have tasted of the sweetness of Thy love." (p. 152). Upborne by this love He counts toil in God's cause to be 'blissful repose,' 'anguish a fountain of gladness.' (p. 136.)

He testifies to the Majesty of the Station held by Him; to the profound and subtle changes in this created world, through which this New Age, the Age of God, was brought into being (p. 295); to the supremacy and triumph of the Revelation (p. 275) and to the eclipse of man's wisdom and the collapse of his power and of his knowledge before the manifest glory and dominion of the Most High. (p. 53.) He gives a picture, unprecedented and unparalleled, of that spiritual illumined world which He is building, the world ordained by God of old which now is to be realised—a world so incomparable to ours that though we read the divine description of it, our aspirations can form as yet no image of its unity, its felicity or its attainments. (Prayers 58, 184, etc.)

One and all, these prayers have for their immediate background and occasion the events of his life and ministry. Dates are not given, nor circumstances. But the prayers evidently cover many dynamic years of intense and extraordinarily varied personal activity—the period during which He regathered the stricken Bábís, reanimated their faith, laid broad and deep in men's hearts the foundations of the Bahá'í Cause, and in spite of successive and accumulating difficulties, in spite of the oppression of priests and tyrants, the machinations of traitors and the lethargy of the public, in spite of sorrows, sufferings and frustrations beyond number, declared His Mission, proclaimed it to the Kings of the World and went down to His last long imprisonment in the city of Acca.

The splendour of His power, His constancy, His spirituality, shines out against the unremitting darkness of His earthly lot. For ever His human self complains and expostulates with Him under the weight of ceaseless affliction: "My blood at all times addresseth Me saying, 'O Thou who art the Image of the Most Merciful! How long will it be ere Thou riddest me of the captivity of this world...?' To this I make reply: 'Be thou patient... The things thou desirest can last but an hour. As to me, ... I quaff continually in the path of God the cup of His decree, and wish not that the ruling of His will should cease to operate . . . Seek thou my wish and forsake thine own'." (p. 11.) His abasement causes His friends to weaken and His enemies to rejoice. Yet He has Himself chosen this suffering (p. 278) and wishes life could be prolonged that He might suffer more for love of God. His afflictions increase His love and His redeeming power. (pp. 146-7). He gives no sign of personal resentment: quite the contrary (p. 307). But He prays for the vindication of the Faithful and the punishment of those who oppose God and His Truth. "Well beloved is Thy mercy unto the sincere among Thy servants, and well beseeming Thy chastisement of the infidels . . . Abase Thou, O my Lord, Thine enemies and lay hold on them with Thy power and might, and let them be stricken by the blast of Thy wrath." (pp. 141, 121.)

Here in this devotional record may be traced the spiritual creation and the first ideal beginnings of the New Age and its glories. Here is fought and won in the heart and soul of the Prophet that battle which established for us the Victory of God on earth. Here is invoked that wrath of an outraged Deity which now overwhelms mankind in its cleansing fires.

As one contemplates the awfulness of the tragedy unfolded in these pages: as one ponders over this intimate revelation of the impassion'd love, the wrongs, the sufferings of Him by Whose stripes we are healed and who for our redemption endured the abominations of the world: the Call to God sounds with a new appeal, and one hears with a new realisation and a new resolve the summons of the All-Victorious.

"Hear Me ye mortal birds! in the Rose Garden of changeless splendour a Flower hath begun to bloom, compared to which every other flower is but a thorn, and before the brightness of Whose glory the very essence of beauty must pale and wither. Arise, therefore, and with the whole enthusiasm of your hearts, . . . of your will, and the concentrated efforts of your entire being, strive to attain the Paradise of His presence, and endeavour to inhale the fragrance of the incorruptible Flower, to breathe the sweet savours of holiness and to obtain a portion of this perfume of celestial glory. Whoso followeth this counsel will break his chains asunder, will taste the abandonment of enraptured love, will attain unto his heart's desire, and will surrender his soul into the hands of his Beloved. Bursting through his cage he will, even as the bird of the Spirit, wing his flight to his holy and everlasting nest.

"Night hath succeeded day and day hath succeeded night, and the hours and moments of your lives have come and gone, and yet none of you hath, for one instant, consented to detach himself from that which perisheth. Bestir yourselves, that the brief moments that are still yours may not be dissipated and lost. Even as the swiftness of lightning your days shall pass and your bodies shall be laid to rest beneath a canopy of dust. What can ye then achieve? How can ye atone for your past failure?

"The everlasting Candle shineth in its naked glory. Behold how it hath consumed every mortal veil. O ye moth-like lovers of His light! brave every danger, and consecrate your souls to its consuming flame. O ye that thirst after Him! strip yourselves of every earthly affection, and hasten to embrace your Beloved. With a zest that none can equal make haste to attain unto Him. The Flower, thus far hidden from the sight of men, is unveiled to your eyes. In the open radiance of His glory He standeth before you. His voice summoneth all the holy and sanctified beings to come and be united with Him. Happy is he that turneth thereunto; well is it with him that hath attained, and gazed on the light of so wondrous a countenance."—(*Gleanings from the Writings of Bahá'u'lláh*, p. 320-22.)

THE LETTERS OF 'ABDU'L-BAHÁ

THESE TABLETS ARE A fountain of heavenly love and joy, of wisdom and power. In every volume, the ceaseless, boundless Love of God pours forth like wine into a thousand different vessels: changing its form, taking the shape of many occasions, filling exactly many needs, but never changing the exquisiteness of its beauty. Love, spontaneous and unstinted, floods every utterance of thought. There is no check, no limit. The days when these letters were written were early days, the days of the first meetings of Lovers and Beloved, the days of God's welcome to the first believers of the western world.

"*This is the time of happiness, the day of rejoicing and of delight.*" (p. 320.) "*With a heart overflowing with the love of God, pray to God in all joy and give Him thanks for this guidance this high gift. Could those who receive these letters but realise the joy with which they are written, they would lift up their hearts and in spirit soar heavenward in exaltation,*" He writes. 'Abdu'l-Bahá at the time of writing these letters was in prison. He was misrepresented, humiliated, frustrated; His life was in danger; difficulties had to be met every hour. Yet no personal distress affects for a moment in the least degree His inward peace of heart or weakens the delight of His fellowship with those who begin to share His love for God.

Whatever sorrow there be in these pages is not for Himself but is through the intensity of His sympathy with the griefs of those to whom He writes. His heart "*is filled with the Love of God, is free and isolated from all save God, is illumined and overflowing with the bounties of the Kingdom of El-Abhá.*" (p. 713.) "*Verily, I am the servant of Bahá'u'lláh, the bond slave of Bahá'u'lláh, the captive of Bahá'u'lláh. I have no grade but this and I do not possess anything for myself.*" (p. 603.)

A power from on high animates Him: the Holy Spirit moves His limbs, His pen. To suffer for God's sake, to drink the cup of sacrifice is His *"utmost hope, the joy of my heart, the consolation of my soul and my final desire."*

Again and again He rejects commiseration offered on account of His calamities and afflictions. *"They are not calamities, but bounties, they are not afflictions but gifts; not hardships, but tranquillity; not trouble, but mercy; and we thank God for this great favour."* (p. 128.) He asserts His independence of all His enemies can do to harm Him.

"I am free," he writes, *"though I should remain in prison; all fortresses and castles cannot confine me, and the dungeon cannot bring me under the narrow bondage of the world. The spirit is ever soaring, even if the body be in the depths . . . Therefore, neither the prison is a cause of sorrow, nor freedom from it a source of joy."* (p. 151.)

These letters fill hundreds of printed pages. Each correspondent is addressed by some special spiritual title chosen by 'Abdu'l-Bahá for him or for her, personally, as, *"Thou Who Art Turning to the Divine Kingdom,"* *"Thou Candle of the Love of God,"* *"Thou Servant of God,"* *"Thou Opened Rose in the Garden of Abhá,"* *"Thou Who Art Awakened to the Cause of God,"* *"Thou Worshipper of Truth,"* *"Thou Servant of Humanity,"* *"Thou Who Art Yearning for the Glad Tidings of God."*

He deals with diverse problems; answers countless questions about the past and the present, about Revelation, about Christianity, about social life, the life of the home, about marriage and children. He sets forth the cause of God and its administration. He exposes the error and the evil of the times. He comforts, counsels, commands, urges; He chants praises of God and of His faithful ones. Whatever the subject, whatever the occasion, whatever the need, the same divine might of His creative love calls into action the awakening spirit of the people of the West. His heart, He writes (p. 60), overflows with gladness and exultation as He reads the letters of the beloved of God whose eyes are enlightened by God, whose hearts and consciences are purified by knowledge and love of God and who have found peace of soul through the commemoration of God.

He remembers them at all times, prays for them every morn

and eve (p. 113) *"Do not think that ye are forgotten for one moment"* (p. 593). *"Trust thou in the love of 'Abdu'l-Bahá, for verily nothing equals it."* (p. 201.)

If for any reason letters do not reach Him He misses them and life and conscience do not find happiness and joy. (p. 375). Yet important and dearly cherished as letters are He is in close and living touch with the faithful in spite of distance, in spite of interruption in correspondence. Time and place do not control the Spirit nor the inwardness of spiritual realities: geographical remoteness from a heavenly centre will not obscure the vision of its glory. *"When the Spirit is breathed in the East its signs immediately appear in the West, and it hath a spiritual dominion which penetrates the pillars of the world."* (p. 289.) If the friends be firm in the cause of God and in His service, spiritual letters come down to them from the Kingdom of Abhá. Their descent is according to an eternal law; their movement is like that of wave following wave and they bear tidings of the unity of God. The love of 'Abdu'l-Bahá for His faithful friends is itself another and a special messenger between them. If a human heart be truly sensitive to the call of God, then there is stretched between its centre and the centre of the Kingdom a connection through which the spirit sends its messages. Every faithful loving heart is endued with this means of communion. (pp. 287, 628.)

'Abdu'l-Bahá is spiritually present with the faithful at their meetings and is their protector, *"spreading His wings over them."* (pp. 90, 282.)

In phrase after phrase, passage after passage challenging, vigorous, profound, He tells of the transcendent unimagined imperishable splendour of the Abhá Kingdom they are entering. (p. 289.)

"O maidservant of God! Every star hath a setting but the star of knowledge of God in the Divine heaven; every light shall darken save the light of the guidance of God; every glory shall vanish away save the glory under the shadow of the word of God." (p. 129.) He calls on the beloved (pp. 411-2) to seize the opportunity God's mercy offers them—*"Truly I say unto you, this is a gift which neither the dominion of the world, nor all the riches of its treasuries,*

nor the glory of its distinguished men, can rival in this resplendent century and new age; inasmuch as crowns are transient but this is eternal and will never be taken away."

"In this material world nothing hath any result, even if it be dominion over the East and the West. But that which hath an immortal result is servitude in the Holy Threshold, service which is rendered to the Kingdom of God and which gives guidance to all on the earth." (p. 424.) *"O beloved of God! know ye that the world is like unto a mirage which the thirsty one thinks to be water . . . Leave it to its people and turn unto the Kingdom of your Lord, the merciful."*

He pours His blessing upon them. *"Blessed are ye, O stars that shine with the light of the love of God! Blessed are ye, O lamps that burn with the fire of love of God. Blessed are ye whose hearts are drawn to the Kingdom. Glad tidings to you who are severed from all save God. . . . Glad tidings to you through the gift of the Covenant . . . Rejoice . . . Be glad . . . Lift up your hearts . . . Let your eyes be solaced by the vision of the bounties of the spiritual Realm."* (p. 30.)

"The cup of knowledge is flowing over, blessed are they who drink of it deeply! . . . The gates of heaven are open, blessed are they who see. The hosts of heaven stand in battle-array—what joy to them who win the victory. The trumpet of life is sounding—how glad the ears of them that hear!" (p. 621.) He calls on them again and again to realise the supreme privilege which is vouchsafed them by the mercy of God, and to pour forth every kind of praise to Him for ever from grateful, happy, radiant hearts. (pp. 182, 259, 413, 594, etc.)

There is a note of warning, too: *"The time is short, and the Divine Courser moves swiftly on."* (p. 406.) To those who complain the path to the Kingdom is hard, obstacles many, difficulties severe; who are perplexed, burdened, discouraged, He says such trials are to be expected. Earthly aims are not won without effort and perseverance, and obstacles to these great spiritual attainments naturally are greater still.

Through steadfastness in overcoming these trials, the soul of the believer is brought nearer to God and at last reaches the condition of knowledge and assurance. As Nature, having borne with patience the lightning and thunderbolts and storms of winters, is afterwards rewarded with the season of blossoms, flowers and fruits; so in the Kingdom of heaven the storms of trials give a constant heart the means of earning the good pleasure of God and the prizes of the Kingdom.

How extreme in times long past were the troubles of the lovers of Christ. Yet their courage was proof, and their reward was eternal life and everlasting Glory.

If tests are severe, it is that they may expose the weakness of those who are unworthy, and enable every true hearted soul to *"shine from the horizon of the Most Great Guidance."* To any such soul tests, however violent, are a gift from God, the Exalted, and He hastens towards them with joy and gladness, for they will cleanse him of those imperfections that keep him removed from his Beloved. (p. 722.)

'Abdu'l-Bahá bids the faithful not to be grieved at the divine trials: but to turn to God, to bow before His will in lowliness, to pray to Him, to be content under all conditions, to be thankful to Him in the midst of affliction.

They are to know that in this age the greatest of all titles, the highest of all praise is given for resolution and firmness because the tests and trials are of the greatest intensity.

The mastery of life and its trials belongs only to believers and comes only from turning to God. When asked about problems of human relationships or the life of the home He affirms that one must at all times be free from merely personal desires and warmed with devotion to God. One must love all people and one's own family with a ray of the infinite Godward love—personal love is not enough.

To one whose home was a place of strain He wrote: *"It behoveth thee to sever thyself from all desires save for thy Lord the supreme, expecting no aid or help from anyone in the Universe, not even thy father or children. Resign thyself to God . . . Be patient. Endure every difficulty and hardship with an uplifted heart, an aspiring spirit, a tongue that delights to make mention of the All-merciful."* (pp. 97-8.) To another He wrote explaining: *"When thou beholdest with the eye of Truth, then thou wilt realise that in this world neither known nor unknown, neither kind father nor beloved son, neither mother nor sister help us. No persons assist except the benevolent Almighty. When thou knowest Him, thou art independent of all else. When thou art attached to His love then thou art detached from kith and kin."* (p. 671.) Only when the heart has broken the lure of a limited love can it be attuned to the perfect love, the perfect joy that will satisfy it for ever.

"Know that in every home where God is praised and prayed to, and His Kingdom proclaimed, that home is a garden of God and a paradise of His happiness." (p. 69.)

He writes of the importance of marriage and of its responsibilities (*e.g.*, pp. 609, 627) and shows (p. 605) that true marriage is accessible only to the spiritually minded, and that the real bond between husband and wife is none other than the Word of God.

He suggests that the naming of a child should be made a religious and social occasion: that friends should be invited to the home and that before the name is given suitable prayers should be said; after which the company should enjoy some light repast together. He calls for obedience and kindness from children to their parents (p. 551); and on the other hand, in the strongest manner, stresses the obligation laid by God in this Dispensation on parents to bring up their children in the knowledge and fear of God. *"Should they neglect this matter they shall be held responsible and worthy of reproach in the presence of the stern Lord. This is a sin unpardonable . . ."* (p. 579.)

For those who seek comfort in the anguish of a fresh bereavement He lifts a little the veil that hides from them that eternal world in which love knows no separation. He bids them remember this parting is limited to the body, its length will be counted in days and over the Spirit death has no dominion at all. Reunion and everlasting consolation are near. *"Thy son shall be with thee in the Kingdom of God and thou shalt behold his smiling face and his brow illumined with the beauty of eternal happiness; then thou wilt have comfort and wilt give thanks to God for His loving kindness to thee."* (p. 86.)

To the faithful or as he names them *"the people of adoration,"* He writes *"death is an ark of deliverance."* (p. 444.) Could these mourners but see in heaven now the faithful souls they lament, wonder and joy would check their tears. He comforts a mourning mother (p. 405.) *"O Bird of the Rose-Garden of Fidelity ! Be of no cheerless heart; have no wing nor feather broken; sigh not, neither do thou wail nor sit chilled in a corner. The little girl lamented is in the divine Rose-Garden in the highest happiness and delight. Why then art thou grieved, sorrowing with a bleeding heart ? This is the day of rejoicing and the hour of ecstassy. This is the season of the spiritually dead coming forth from their graves and gathering together. This is the promised time for the attainment of plenteous grace.*

"Be calm, be strong, be grateful, and become a lamp full of light, that the darkness of sorrow may be scattered and the sun of everlasting joy arise in brilliant splendour from the dawning place of heart and soul. Upon thee be the Glory of the Most Glorious !"

To a physician seeking counsel, He writes (p. 688): *"Whenever thou presentest thyself at the bed of a patient turn thy face towards the Lord of the Kingdom and supplicate assistance from the Holy Spirit and heal the ailments of the sick one."* (p. 685.)

Answering an enquiry about the nature of the sympathetic nervous system He explains that the powers of the sympathetic nerve are not exclusively spiritual nor exclusively physical, but are between the two and connected with both. The operation of the nerve is normal when its relations with the spiritual and the physical systems are perfect. *"When the material and the divine world are rightly co-related, when the hearts become heavenly and the aspirations grow pure and divine, then perfect connection between the two systems will follow. Then shall this power be shown in its perfection, and physical and spiritual diseases shall receive complete healing. The exposition is brief. Ponder, and thou shall understand the meaning."* (p. 309.)

All life in reality opens on heaven, and all experience lies in the path of God. To those who consult Him about the study and practice of letters, music, painting, science and the like, 'Abdu'l-Bahá explains that these pursuits are one and all to be inspired by the sense of worship. *"Art is worship,"* as He once said. He affirms that a spiritual motive in the artist will quicken his progress and heighten his proficiency. A believer will find his art a natural medium of communicating the Divine Message; if his work has itself a spiritual quality it will awaken the spiritual susceptibilities of the beholder while his social intercourse with fellow-artists will tend to guide their thoughts to appreciation of the Divine Beauty. (pp. 449-50.)

At the present time all divine power poured from heaven on humanity has its focus in Bahá'u'lláh, and reaches mankind through His mediation alone. As in our solar system the source of all physical light is the sun, and every light directly or indirectly is derived from it, so in the spiritual realm every Age has its Messiah and truth is attained by men only through Him. (p. 592.) "*Whatever question thou hast in thy heart,*" writes 'Abdu'l-Bahá, "*turn thou thy heart towards the kingdom of Abhá and entreat at the threshold of the Almighty and reflect upon that problem; then unquestionably the light of Truth shall dawn and the reality of that problem will become evident and clear to thee. For the teachings of His Highness Bahá'u'lláh are the keys to all the doors.*" (p. 692.)

In the past, He points out, there were great philosophers who upheld the ideal of the oneness of humanity; but at that time the support and inspiration of heaven were not forthcoming so that their endeavours bore no fruit. To-day there are many souls in the world who spread thoughts of peace and reconciliation and long to establish the unity of the human race. But they likewise are without the dynamic power to carry their ideal into effect. This power belongs only to the instructions and exhortations of Bahá'u'lláh whose summons to world-unity is supported by the word of God and by all the resources of the Kingdom of the Most High. "*Therefore, O thou lover of the oneness of the world of humanity, spread thou as much as thou canst the instructions and teachings of His Highness Bahá'u'lláh.*" (p. 691.)

There is indeed need of a thousand teachers, He writes, each one severed from the world, attracted by the Holy Spirit, radiant with the joy of the Kingdom, seeking no reward or recompense. "*Strive with life and guide the people to the Kingdom of God, lead them to the straight pathway, inform them of the greatness of the Cause and give them the glad tidings.*" (p. 360.)

The world of humanity to-day is like a sick and feeble man; the teachers are wise physicians. The remedies which they are to apply are two. The first to be given is that of guidance, that the people "*may turn unto God, hearken to the divine commandments and go forth with a hearing ear and a seeing eye.*" When this remedy has had its effect, then the people are "*to be trained in the conduct, morals and deeds of the Supreme Concourse, encouraged and inspired with the gifts of the Kingdom of Abhá.*" (pp. 36-7.) Their hearts are to be cleansed of all ill-will and to be strengthened in all the attributes of love and union so that East and West may be joined in one, and universal peace be established. In the pursuit of their task, teachers are not to spare themselves nor to seek rest. They are to make the utmost endeavour to bring the Glad Tidings to the ears of mankind and are to accept every calamity and affliction in their love for God and their reliance on 'Abdu'l-Bahá. (p. 38.) They are to drink from the eternal chalice of the love of God, to enjoy its ecstasy and in the radiance of the beauty of Abhá be all aglow with zeal, delight and eager energy. They all are to work together in perfect unanimity and singleness of purpose. "*Ye must attain such spiritual unity and agreement that ye may express one spirit and one life.*" (p. 23.)

It was to this end, to unite the hearts of the beloved of God, that Bahá'u'lláh endured all difficulties and all ordeals (p. 247); and the aim of 'Abdu'l-Bahá's devotion and service is the same; "*that union and affection may be created among the beloved of God, nay the whole of the human world.*" (p. 421.)

Nothing can exceed the emphasis and earnestness with which in these Tablets he appeals for concord and unity among believers. This is the vital instrument through which is to be achieved the master-objective of the Bahá'í Movement, namely the transforming of the earth into a paradise, the wide world into one home, the nations of East and West into one household. "*Not until this (union) is realised will the cause advance by any means whatsoever.*" Therefore, even in those early days of the Faith when believers were very few in the West, He begins the work of organisation, urges co-operation and gatherings among the friends, the forming of committees for promoting the Cause and of what were at that

time called Boards of Consultation. "*The greatest means for the
union and harmony of all is Spiritual Meetings. This matter is very
important.*" (p. 125.)

Such meetings will be magnets drawing down divine strength.

"*Blessed are ye,*" He writes to one group, "*for organising the
assembly of unity.*" As these meetings begin to materialise, He
insists that the highest degree of union and harmony must exist
between them. The spiritual meeting of consultation in New York
must be in the fullest accord with that in Chicago, and when a
similar meeting "*shall be organised in Washington, these two
meetings of Chicago and New York must be in unity and harmony
with that meeting.*"

He watches over the constitution of these bodies, instructs that
each shall have its clearly marked purpose and fit into the general
scheme as an integral part of the whole, and that no spirit of
exclusiveness shall be aroused such as has happened in earlier
Dispensations when arrangements which "*were in the beginning a
means for harmony became in the end a cause of trouble.*" (p. 394.)

He enjoins, too, the great observance of the Faith, the yearly
fast from March 2nd-20th; "*the nineteen-day Fast is a duty to be
observed by all*" (p. 57)—and the "*Feast of Remembrance or
Meeting of Faithfulness*" as it was then called (p. 421).

"*This Feast,*" He writes (p. 468), "*was established by His
Highness The Báb, to occur once in nineteen days. Likewise the
Blessed Perfection hath commanded, encouraged and reiterated it.
Therefore, it hath the utmost importance. Undoubtedly you must
give the greatest attention to its establishment and raise it to the
highest point of importance, so that it may become continual and
constant.*"

He then gives directions as to the keeping of the Feast; and
concludes—"*If the Feast is arranged in this manner and in the way
mentioned, that supper is the Lord's supper, for the result is the same
result and the effect is the same effect.*" (pp. 468-9.)

These Tablets, published in America and written chiefly to
American believers, form a sister—and complementary—volume
to that which contains 'Abdu'l-Bahá's American addresses and
bears the title *The Promulgation of Universal Peace*. Taken

together they form, as it were, a complete circle of Divine and practical instruction for the times.

The Addresses constitute the profoundest and most comprehensive textbook on modern problems. They reveal what true modernism is, dealing with the larger aspects of the Cause of Bahá'u'lláh, with questions of the relations and the history of religions and of peoples, with science and philosophy, with the principles of world order and with definite plans for its establishment. The Tablets, on the other hand, are directed for the most part to individuals, often to individuals who look to Him with ardent belief and adoring love. They reveal clearly and emphatically the essential nature of His own special station as the bondservant of Bahá'u'lláh and the Centre of the Covenant. They are heart to heart talks on the personal hopes and aspirations of His correspondents, their personal trials and difficulties, their personal duties and obligations to God and His Faith. The writer's attitude is that of a host greeting an honoured and loved guest, a father welcoming a dear son home from a long and perilous journey: it is that of a divine messenger who brings to those struggling in the uncertain turmoil of earthly life a foretaste of the sweetness and fragrance and harmony and peace of Paradise and of the eternal glory and power that will be the reward of victory.

'Abdu'l-Bahá stated that these Tablets have an importance which will not be appreciated for many long years to come. But perhaps their message of the impassioned all-embracing love of God will never be more sadly needed than it is now, nor more precious than it is to us as we battle on through the heart of the storm and the darkness and the ruin of the Night of Judgment and Retribution.

THE WELLSPRING OF HAPPINESS

I

HAPPINESS IS OUR birthright: it is ours to take, to hold, to possess in perpetuity. If it seem hidden from us it is not hidden by distance but by nearness. We do not have to go questing for it through the wide earth nor through the immensity of the heavens. It is in our midst. It is closer to us than breathing. It is buried in our own heart's-deep, deep in the heart's inmost recesses; and there it dwells waiting to be recognised, to be discovered.

Everyone can be happy and ought to be. God expects it and enjoins it. Every Revelation comes as Glad Tidings, bidding man be glad and giving him cause to be. Every Prophet has found men wandering in sadness and misery and has rebuked them for it. He has called them away from the things that produce unhappiness from anxiety and worry and cupidity, from fear of the future, from anticipation of evil, from lack of hope and faith. He has opened to them a way of escape, promised them deliverance from evil, and the attainment, by God's grace, of a happiness that will satisfy and endure. Now in our time the Prophet of the New Age into which we are entering, Bahá'u'lláh, gives once again the ancient glad tidings—tidings of a happiness poured forth from heaven on all men everywhere in even greater abundance, yes, in far, far greater abundance than ever in the history of the past—a happiness the bright and eager intensity of which can only be measured, if at all, by the bitterness of our need and by the extremity of our humiliation and our suffering. Exultation and victory ring in every sentence of His proclamation of the All-Glorious Advent of God. The ancient promise, He cries, is fulfilled.

God's mercy and generosity have overcome at last the apathy and dullness of His creatures. His Name has conquered the earth. He has exposed to man's knowledge the futility and the stupidity of strife. The long power of delusion is broken. The reign of violence and misery is doomed. The time has come for man to attain a new understanding, new ideals, a new life which will deliver him permanently from the glooms and superstitions of ignorance and will make possible that serene divine happiness which he was created to enjoy. The earth (throughout its entire length and breadth) ought now to be filled with songs of praise and thanksgiving; and the only reason it is not so is that the opacity of man's pride has shut out from his knowledge the light of the joy of heaven that is beating upon him.

'Abdul-Bahá taught that one of the nine marks by which the True Messenger of God was to be identified was His being "*a joy bringer and the herald of the kingdom of happiness.*" Bahá'u'lláh in the midst of dire afflictions showed forth a spirit of serenity and acceptance radiating in others that deep steadfast joy that filled His own heart. He taught men to think of God as a God of Bliss—as one "*by whose name the sea of joy moveth and the fragrances of happiness are wafted.*" He bade men if they wished for happiness to pray for it to God.

"*Vouchsafe me of Thy bounty that which will brighten my eyes and gladden my heart . . .*" "*Grant me the joy of beholding Thy eternal Being, O Thou who dwellest in my inmost heart . . .*" "*Send down upon me the fragrant breezes of Thy joy.*"

He bade men receive His message as a summons to happiness. "*O Son of Spirit! with the joyful tidings of light I hail thee: rejoice! . . . The spirit of holiness beareth unto thee joyful tidings of reunion; wherefore dost thou grieve? O Son of man! Rejoice in the gladness of thine heart, that thou mayest be worthy to meet Me and to mirror Forth My Beauty.*"

'Abdu'l-Bahá brought to the world the message of the New Revelation as Glad Tidings. "*If,*" He would say, "*this does not make you happy, what is there that will make you happy?*" A man ought to be happy because if he were not he could not be in the frame of mind to receive the bounties poured forth from on high.

When He gave a direction to the English Bahá'ís for the keeping of the day of the Báb, "*the day of the dawning of the heaven of Guidance,*" His words were: "*Be happy—be happy—be full of*

Joy!" On another occasion, He said, "*The people must be so attracted to you that they will exclaim, 'What happiness exists among you?' and will see in your faces the lights of the Kingdom; then in wonderment they will turn to you and seek the cause of your happiness.*"

When asked to describe how true believers ought to live, His first direction was that they should cause no one any unhappiness; and He closed His adjuration with a kindred thought—"*Be a cause of healing for every sick one, a comforter for every sorrowful one, a pleasant water for every thirsty one, a star to every horizon, a light for every lamp, a herald to every one who yearns for the Kingdom of God.*"

In the days of persecution in Persia, so great a spirit of happiness pervaded the Bahá'ís that it was said one could not take tea with them without wishing to join their society; and so strong was their personal influence that their enemies believed them to be possessed of some unholy magic by which they won the hearts of men to believe in the new doctrine. We have for so long sought happiness by secular or even pagan ways that although these are leading us to a dead end, we find it hard to admit that we have been travelling altogether in the wrong direction. Religion (for all the honours we instinctively pay it) has in the hands of traditionalists and formalists proved itself so impotent, a cause of so much division and discord, that when once again for the first time in hundreds and hundreds of years a Divine Prophet stands in our midst and in the name of God offers deliverance and peace of heart and blessedness we can hardly believe our eyes or our ears.

We refuse to recognise that a clue to the most precious of all lost secrets has been put into our hands and that the mystery of a perfect love has been opened to us. The very lavishness and immensity of the gift bewilders us, almost stupefies us; as though a beggar had asked a crust and was given a kingdom. The timeliness of the gift still further enhances its value and magnifies our astonishment.

Religion has become more and more discredited. Its results have not seemed at all worth its disciplines. Its views on life have grown antiquated and do not fit nor illumine modern conditions of society. Those who appeared as the protagonists of religion have not stood out as models of happiness or broad sympathies: they have not been able to give men any clear guidance in the moral mazes of modern existence nor to impart comfort or strength in the frustrations that beset our efforts at stablising the social order.

Men have found many excuses for letting their faith grow cold and their religious sense become atroph'ed by disuse. Ordinary everyday human life has become so varied, so rich, so full of change and of movement and of novelty that it seems to be quite full and satisfying in itself and to stand in no need of religion. Men find full employment and room for intense and engrossing activities in purely secular and mundane interests. Never have they acquired so much to gratify their pride; never have they been so equipped to refine and elaborate their pleasures. They sought happiness altogether in the material things that lay to their hand.

And to a large extent—they found it!

God is kind and generous. He has made it easier for man to be happy than to be unhappy. He has scattered some kind or other of pleasantness for us everywhere. No one can miss it all! Songs of celestial delight, fragrances from the Gardens of Paradise, rays of some beatific Beauty are borne to earth on all the winds of heaven and cause some echo, however brief, some reflection, dim or faint; or find some home in the hearts of men wherein to rest. We sharpened our intellects, cast away our superstitions and obscurations of the past, unearthed the secrets of nature, appropriated her powers and extended our control over the world about us in a manner in which our ancestors, even a century ago, would never have imagined to be possible. Never had so complex and so forceful a civilisation been reared upon the face of the earth. And if we were compelled to feel there was something incomplete and insecure about it all; if we realised the tiger and the ape in us had not been outgrown, and if we saw that in spite of ourselves we were sinking back to the primitive ways of the jungle; nevertheless, no earlier generation of men had found so much in the world to amuse and divert and flatter and gratify them, or to

D

prove so clearly their supremacy over all the lower forms of creation. If all civilised beings were not supermen they were assuredly superanimals and had at command a thousand kinds of intellectual entertainment which were peculiarly human and their own. Men explored the resources of humanism and bathed their souls and their sense in its delights. Intellectuals discounted that part of our tradition which is derived from Israel and emphasised more and more that which has come down to us from Greece. They turned, not their hearts only, but their minds, too, from their religious inheritance to an inheritance that was definitely not religious but artistic and literary. The Greeks carved statues of their gods which remain to this day models of taste and skill and are the envy and admiration of the world: but these gods were assuredly not made to be worshipped. The Greeks reared the Parthenon and countless temples, which are in their kind masterpieces as perfect as their works of sculpture. But these temples do not suggest the unseen world; they do not carry with them an air of mystery, of awe, of exultation. Contrast them with a Christian cathedral—with that sense of distance, with that sublimity and aspiration which the soaring lines of Gothic awake in the spectator's soul—and the limitation of the Greek architect at once is betrayed. A Greek temple with its flat lines is of the earth, earthy: "A table on four legs: a dull thing," as William Morris is said to have exclaimed of the Parthenon: and he was no belittler of the beauty of the past.

No one would disparage the glory that was Greece nor yet the splendour that was Rome. All the encomiums passed upon them recently by scholars are no doubt as just as they are enthusiastic. But the most significant thing about the revival of Greek influence is that its champions attribute that revival to the fact that the Greek world was non-religious and purely humanistic and that its affinity which connects our age with theirs lies in the common limitations of both. In neither does the spiritual seek to find expression. Revelation was unknown to the Greeks and is unacceptable to the modern: hence they say in our outlook on life we are akin.

One of the greatest authorities on Greek humanism, Professor

R. W. Livingstone, a brilliant and charming writer, puts the point quite clearly in his book *Greek Genius and Its Meaning to Us.* "Let us sum up," he says, "the reasons of our approximation to Greece. First is Greek humanism . . . The Greek set himself to answer the question how with no revelation from God to guide him . . . man should live. It has been a tendency in our own age either to deny that heaven has revealed to us in any way how we ought to behave or to find such a revelation in human nature itself. In either case we are thrown back on ourselves and obliged to seek our guide there. That is why the influence of Greece has grown so much. The Greeks are the only people who have conceived the problem similarly; their answer the only one that has yet been made."

That is very clear. But who will affirm that the masterpieces inspired by the Christian religion are less splendid than those of Greek humanism? Who will deny that Christian literature and art, in all its branches, the work of men as various as Michael Angelo and Milton, and Dante and da Vinci, has a beauty and a power and a richness and a majesty even superior to that of Greeks—and to what is this due but manifestly and confessedly to a spiritual revelation?

Whatever masterpieces of humanistic art and craftsmanship the Greeks may have left us, did they bequeath to posterity any secret of happiness—of a happiness that really satisfies, leaving no hunger, a happiness that endures producing no satiety and not ending at the last in something that is not happiness? And those academicians who drank deeply of the fountain of Greek wisdom, have they been able to save us from this self-stultification of intellectualism?

Is there to be found in Greek literature or art anything comparable to that high, noble, courageous, invincible joy that vibrates in a book which formally is by no means a Greeklike masterpiece of artistic skill or genius—the New Testament?

It was the Greeks who handed down to us the story of the Skeleton at the Feast and told how before the banquet closed a servant would bring a skeleton and bid the guests "eat, drink and be merry for to-morrow you die." It was the Greeks who said no man should be called happy till his death, and they certainly did not promise him much happiness beyond it. Not to live long, they thought, was best; those whom the gods loved died young. The most wonderful and famous of their literary works gave no message of glory and hope and triumph, but were tragedies, written frequently around themes of a sombre, terrifying and even gruesome cast.

Scholars have remarked that an undertone of sadness seemed to run through the great literature of Greece. The reason is that it is humanistic—and nothing more. For when humanism thinks deeply, it thinks sadly. Our English Renaissance was not so secular as was the culture of ancient Greece: far from it. England was a Christian country with a Christian tradition and the Authorised Version was produced at the same time as *The Tempest* and *The Winter's Tale*. But the accent of its Renaissance was on the human not the spiritual side, and Shakespeare in this was a true exponent of it. Broad as his sympathies were, if there be any character he could not have understood nor have put sympathetically into a drama, it is such a one as Shelley. You will find many notes in Shakespeare's singing; but not the note of the poetry of Blake. Shakespeare's world was far from being as Revelationless as that of ancient Greece; but the mystical aspect of things is not brought into his picture.

He, too, when he thought deeply, thought sadly. His greatest works are not his comedies, brilliant as these are. Even in these there is a shadow: not only in *The Merchant of Venice* but even in the gayest of all, *Twelfth Night* and *As You Like It*, and still more in *The Tempest*. (Poor Prospero: at the end he must bury his art—not carry it on to happier fulfilment!) But his greatest works were his tragedies and his fame rests on them.

How mighty and vigorous, how confident, adventurous, and triumphant was the England of those days, the England of Queen Elizabeth! Yet that eager and self-sufficient age did not through its most eloquent spokesmen speak the fullest happiness. Could any illustration show more conclusively the inadequacy of humanism to meet the needs of humanity?

However gay, delightful, praiseworthy, the happiness that

humanism fathers, it must in the nature of things be qualified. It cannot be complete. Humanism can only bid us make the best of things—to look on the bright side and take the rough with the smooth. But sorrow and suffering cannot be ignored or evaded. They will insistently intrude themselves. It is not the stoic who has overcome the world and is able to bequeath his joy to others when he is gone. No, sorrow and suffering must be faced and included within the scheme of happiness: there is no device by which they can be left on the outside of life and induced to remain there! And if this alternation of shadow and light, this chequered and inconstant happiness be the best that life can give; if our well-being be the sport of circumstance and the plaything of fate, then, indeed, one can hardly escape from pessimism. The birds of the air who neither have to sow nor reap are happier than we!

It is religion which teaches us that pessimism is utterly wrong; that pessimism is the product of a circumscribed and limited experience. It is religion which for the first time opens up to man's vision the height and depth, the range and the reality of God's munificence to His creatures.

God has created man other sources of pleasure and happiness which lie beyond those of reason and the senses; He has created solaces, delights, raptures which arise out of the activity of higher powers, higher faculties, and belong to man's moral nature, to the inmost and most real sphere of his being. The sphere of conscience, of the sense of right and wrong, of spiritual perception, has been affirmed by God and is felt instinctively by man to be of greater value and dignity, to be farther from earth and nearer to heaven, than the realm of sensibility or ratiocination; and the content, the tranquility, the happiness, the ecstasy that attach to it (like, too, its pains) are more deeply set and more vital than those which derive from the lower ranges of man's consciousness. The common everyday experience of every mortal being bears witness to this truth; and the long, glorious story of those who in every age have laboured to advance civilisation, to promote moral progress, to establish the practice of true religion, is rich in proofs of it.

II

Of a surety God is Joy! This is the creed, the experience, the message of religion. Not only high poets through their intuition, but the seers, the saints, the prophets, one and all, have recognised this all-explanatory, this all-animating truth. The hopes and dreams of suffering, longing mankind have been as a mirror reflecting a great reality. There is—there is a Being whose name is Bliss—changeless, throned above vicissitude and all shadow, without beginning or ending, the Eternal One, the Master of all Life, radiant, beautiful, beloved!

Had they not known this Being, the Founders of the Religions could never have thought or spoken or endeavoured as they did: they would have had no message of comfort to give to sorrowing mankind and they could not have promised that all tears would be wiped away and only happiness would remain. Christ Himself possessed inalienably this joy; and the immortal prospect which He held before those who died in the faith was that of sharing in eternity the joy of God. One of His express gifts to His disciples on earth was joy. *"These things I have spoken unto you that my joy may be within you and your joy complete."* He said that the joy of the true believer was so great that for joy he would sell all he had to gain the object of his love! And He assured His disciples that nothing would ever take this joy away from them. The disciples are described as being filled with joy and the Holy Spirit. Paul described the Kingdom of God as "joy in the Holy Ghost," and bade those to whom he wrote to "Rejoice in the Lord," and "evermore to give thanks." The New Testament, not only in the Gospels, but from the Acts to the Apocalypse, is alive with the spirit of a pervading and inviolable joy.

Not in the New Testament only but in the higher reaches of the Old Testament the same song of happiness is heard: "Rejoice in the Lord, O ye righteous: for praise is comely for the righteous." "I will greatly rejoice in the Lord, my soul shall be joyful in my God."

Had not the early Christians been animated with an invincible confidence and an amazing power of attraction, they could never have overcome indifference and persecution and won the hearts of the world to submission to Christ.

One striking proof of this spirit meets one in the early works of Christian art. This art was largely a sepulchral art, found in the catacombs or associated with death and often with martyrdom; and it was produced in time of tribulation and struggle. Yet images of sorrow and suffering are systematically excluded from it, nor is there in it any expression of bitterness or complaint. Pictures such as that of Daniel unharmed among the lions or the three children unscathed amid the flames, are the sole indication of the dreadful persecutions raging at the time. There are few representations of martyrdom, and none (as it seems) till a late date. Instead, one finds emblems of beauty and happiness— pictures of the miracles of mercy, sweet emblems of immortality, and even joyous images borrowed from the mythology of the pagans.

Centuries passed away before this brave and tender note ceased to be dominant in Christian art and another and very different mood took its place.

In distant India, long before the time of Christ, the Gita had borne witness to their Eternal Joy and had opened to men the way to realise it.

"For persons free from desire or hatred, for the persons who have controlled their mind and who have realised the Self every-where is found the bliss of Brahman."

And again, *"To persons who have known the Self, the bliss of Brahman lies everywhere."*

Buddha uttered statements similar to those of Christ on His possession and His gift of happiness. He said of Himself that He *"lived in the pure land of eternal bliss even while he was still in the body and he preached the laws of religion to you and the whole world that you and your brethren may attain the same peace and the same happiness."*

He set forth five meditations through the use of which the devotee might reach the land of bliss, the first of love, the second of pity, *"the third of joy in which you think of the prosperity of others and rejoice with their rejoicings."*

Buddha taught insistently that misery and fear were caused by error, and that knowledge of truth conferred a complete and undying joy even here on earth.

"There is misery in the world of birth and death: there is much misery and pain. But greater than all the misery is the bliss of truth . . . Blessed is he who has become an embodiment of truth and loving kindness. He conquers though he may be wounded; he is glorious and happy, although he may suffer . . ."

"This is the sign that a man follows the right path: Uprightness is his delight and he sees danger in the least of the things which he should avoid. He trains himself in the commands of morality, he encompasseth himself with holiness in word and deed . . . mindful and self-possessed, he is altogether happy." And again: *"A brother who with firm determination walks in the noble path is sure to come forth in the light, sure to reach up to the higher wisdom, sure to attain to the highest bliss of enlightenment."*

But all the Founders of Religion have taught that the way to truth and the joy of truth is narrow and difficult. The Divine Being who is the Soul of Bliss is hard to find, hard to attain to. Objects of earthly ambition are not gained without perseverance and labour: how much more effort will then be needed to achieve this blissful union which is the most precious and the final goal of all human endeavour! This divine joy is closely hidden, jealously concealed from the casual observation of man—but it is not hidden by distance. On the contrary, it lies close at hand and if it cannot be seen, this is because it is so very near. Not only is it, as the poet said of God, "nearer to us than breathing, closer than hands and feet" (that would be wonderful enough); but it is nearer to us than we are to ourselves. There is in human nature always a possibility that a man's superstition or self-illusion will hang a veil between himself and his heart so that he will be in blank ignorance of that which lies at the centre of his own being.

*"Their superstitions have become veils between them and their own hearts and kept them from the path of God, the Exalted, the Great."**

---

*Bahá'u'lláh: *Tablet of Ahmad*

The psychological make-up of a man may be likened to a figure consisting of three or four concentric circles, the outer representing his body and the senses, the next representing the mental realm, the next the moral realm, and the innermost circle standing for the realm of the spiritual which is the essential part of man, the heart of his heart, and soul of his soul. It is possible for a man to live and move and spend his whole existence in the outer fringes of his being, to shut away from his experience the finer activities of thought and feeling and to have his nobler and most vital faculties misused. He may occupy his time in this or that pursuit yet never effect an entry into the sphere of conscience, of faith, or of spirit.

Such men, said Christ, are dead. Though they walk about and work and wield earthly influence, though they govern a province or preside at a Sanhedrin, they are only rational animals, men in an embryonic stage, unfit to be dignified by the title "man" in the fullness of its meaning. Such men cannot be happy. Their minds are operating in a sphere where a stable and satisfying happiness is not to be had. They are unconscious of that finer and inner realm of being in which happiness is to be sought and found. Not to such men but to His disciples did Jesus leave His peace and His joy.

This communion with God through which a man finds Bliss is a communion of love, a meeting of like with like.

"*I have breathed within thee a breath of My own spirit, that thou mayest be My lover.*" *

When the veils of illusion which hide a man's own heart from himself are drawn aside, when after purgation he comes to himself and attains self-knowledge and sees himself as he truly is, then at the same moment and by the same act of knowledge he beholds there in his own heart His Father who has patiently awaited His son's return.

Only through this act of self-completion, through this conclusion of the journey which begins in the kingdom of the senses and leads inward through the kingdom of the moral to end in that of the spiritual, does real happiness become possible. Now

---

* Bahá'u'lláh: *The Hidden Words*

for the first time a man's whole being can be integrated, and a harmony of all his faculties be established. Through his union with the Divine Spirit he has found the secret of the unifying of his own being. He who is the Breath of Joy becomes the animating principle of his existence. Man knows the Peace of God.

This union with God is the only happiness which the Prophets one and all affirm as worthy of the name. It does not belong to the accidents of life and is in no degree the product of imagination or illusion. It is independent of all contingencies. It rests on direct perception, on immediate union between the creature and his Creator. It is shared with God in its essence and is therefore imperishable and secure. The world did not give it and the world cannot take it away. Afflictions may add to its strength and intensity, as winds will blow a glowing fire to a flame; but they cannot violate it. It does not deny the other and lesser pleasures which God in His generosity has bestowed upon His creatures. It does not subsist on their mortification. It is compatible with them all. It does not demand asceticism. The ministry of Jesus began with a marriage feast and His enemies accused Him of being a gluttonous man and a wine-bibber. The Great Ones of the Bahá'í Revelation lived, so far as conditions permitted, normal human lives. As sons and brothers, as husbands and fathers, and friends and men of business and affairs, they set examples which men may look to as they follow the ordinary course of social life. Bahá'u'lláh expressly discouraged ascetic habits: "*take what God has given you*," He said. He permitted men by definite injunction to enjoy the comforts and comelinesses and even the luxuries of life so long as these did not wean their hearts from servitude to God and the informing spirit of sacrifice. The ordinary pleasures of life, material and intellectual, are to be taken as they come, neither being sought nor avoided but left to fall into their appropriate places.

There is only one peace of mind, one joy, one happiness which in itself deserves to be an object of contemplation and desire. The Great Prophets are not content merely to bear witness to the reality of this, or to describe its nature. They do more; they bear it into the world as a gift; they bring it within men's reach, urge and encourage them to seek for it till they find it. The imperative which they lay on men: "*Rejoice and be exceeding glad, for great is your reward in heaven . . .*" is not a mere counsel of perfection, not (God forbid) an unkind command to seek a goal which men cannot attain (—will God mock His creatures ?). It is a promise of success. "*Seek and ye shall find: knock and it shall be opened to you*"; which is as if He said, "You have only to strive and you will attain."

"*The heavens of Thy mercy and the oceans of Thy bounty are so vast Thou hast never disappointed those who will come to Thee.*" *

The poet does much when he testifies that God is Joy and when he, with inspired vision, paints scenes of elysian beatitude that await the aspiring soul of man. The High-Prophet does yet more. He opens not a vision, but the truth itself. He brings the truth down into the world among men. He imparts to those ready to receive it, the power to know the truth and become one with it.

Tragically every Prophet in religious history has found only a very few persons ready to accept Him and faithfully to follow out His directions. Neither in His life-time, nor in the life-time of the religion which He founds, though this be centuries long, are there many disciples who will really put His commandments to the test, will persevere in whole-hearted and exact obedience and continue in spite of discouragements in the way He has marked out till they reach the goal. Spiritual lassitude, moral compromise, the substitution of the formal for the essential, have been the rule in the history of all religions. In consequence the general effect of the teaching of the Prophets has only been a fraction of what it might have been. The possibilities of religion, as affirmed by those to whom the religions owe their origin, have never been developed. The proportion of informed and determined followers to the total population was never considerable enough to produce large historic results. There never have been many who sought their happiness in the spiritual sphere and found that road to inward bliss which their Prophet had trodden and had left open wide for them to walk in. The efforts of men and nations, even too often of churches, have been bent in other directions and

* Bahá'u'lláh: *A Prayer*

their energies have been spent on less immaterial objects. In consequence, human history all the world over has been darkened with troubles and vicissitudes that need never have been, and has never been blessed with the hope, the vision, the sense of proportion, or with anything better than the least suggestion of the well being and happiness which the Prophet had brought within human reach.

Not only the facts of history but the recorded forecasts of the Prophets in their lifetime bear witness to this. Moses and Jesus both foresaw the failures and the sufferings of their followers. No Scripture seems to show such premonitions of future disasters and calamities or contains so many and such grave warnings of faithlessness and of tribulation to come as the Gospel. But even in our own Age Bahá'u'lláh Himself warned men of dire retribution at hand:

"*O Ye Peoples of the World! Know verily that an unforeseen calamity is following you and that grievous retribution awaiteth you. Think not the deeds ye have committed have been blotted from My sight.*" But if the great world never yet has grasped or perceived its blessings and if the Prophets have foreseen and foretold these ineptitudes and failures, the Prophets with one consent from the first to the last, from the mythic times of Adam to the present ere have assured mankind in no uncertain tones that this frustration and misery would not last forever. The day would come when the religious and social conviction of mankind would be changed, when the reality of spiritual happiness would be appreciated, if not by the whole human race, at least by great and prevailing multitudes and when it would become the possession not of a very, very few, but of very many.

From the beginning, the date of this Event has been fixed by the providence of the Creator. From the beginning, the certainty of its future advent has been foretold to man in every Revelation. A symbolic reference to it is recorded in the first chapter of the Bible, when the seventh or final day of creation is shown as different from all the earlier days, as distinctively the Day of completeness and of divine rest, the Day of God. Only one Prophet—among all the Prophets—has not foretold this future

Day of Fulfilment and Happiness: Bahá'u'lláh. His pronouncement is more triumphant and happy, far more than that of any
who preceded Him—for His Glad Tidings is that the Promised
Day of Happiness has come! God has come in the plenitude of His
power and the Lord of Bliss has established His kingdom on
earth. At last God's love for His creatures has prevailed over man's
resistance. God's Name has conquered the earth. Man is to lift
his eyes from mundane levels and to look up towards heavenly
places. His consciousness is to expand. The fires of love are to be
kindled in his heart and spiritual impulses are to stir and move
his soul. He is to become aware of the spiritual realms that have
lain unexplored in the recesses of his own heart and mind. He is
to turn his eyes within, upon himself, and to find God Himself
standing there powerful, mighty, supreme—the Lord of Joy.

To-day is the end of man's long journey. The prodigal after
his wanderings and his humiliations has come to himself. He
knows at last what he is; and whence he came. He has returned to
the Father who has left His own Home and come to meet the
beloved on the way. It is the Day of Reunion; the Day of God's
fulfilment, the Day of Joy. And that Blissful Being with whom
man is now joined again, is found not to have absented Himself
from man, not to have hidden Himself, in the heights nor in the
depths, but to have been at hand, radiant and glorious in the
recesses of man's own spiritual being.

THE GENIUS OF IRELAND

O NCE, AND ONLY ONCE, and for One only has Ireland taken the part of a leader among the peoples of Europe. Save for this one historical achievement, she has stood outside the main currents of development in the West, and has mingled little in European affairs. During the sixth, seventh and eighth centuries, and later, she played an illustrious part in the propagation of Christianity in Europe, and won for herself the undying title of the Island of Saints and Scholars. From the distant Age until recent times, she has been overwhelmed by invaders whom her rich lands attracted, and has had to endure the suppression of much that was most precious in her peculiar individuality. Now, when another Age of moral darkness has fallen upon mankind, she is coming at last to her own and has begun to give expression to her most noble gifts: and now, by the kind providence of God, another opportunity is offered her of doing again for mankind the high service she did once in centuries long gone by.

That service was intellectual and spiritual. It made Irish history during the sixth, seventh and eighth centuries a conspicuous part of religious European history. It won for her that title of the Island of Saints and Scholars, which remains to prove that Ireland was not always in that sad spiritual plight in which she seems to be to-day.

The chief features of that age of light are well known. From many parts of Europe students thronged into Ireland to sit at the feet of Irish Professors and Divines, and Irish teachers travelled over sea and land to bring the gift of heavenly and of earthly knowledge to yet unilluminated regions of Britain and the Continent.

The three patron saints of Ireland, St. Patrick, St. Bridget and Columcille, founded schools at Armagh, Kildare and in Iona. Hundreds followed their example. Shrines of devotion and of learning were established in every part of the island. St. Finnian, travelling in Britain and seeing the ignorance of the people, planned their conversion, and returning to Ireland founded at Clonard that famous school whose students during his lifetime numbered three thousand. Moville, Bangor, Lismore, Cork, Ross, Glendalough, Innisfallen, were seats of noted colleges. Districts now looked on in Ireland as remote were then educational centres whose circumference might reach as far as France or Italy. The lonely island of Aran Mor, in the days of its great teacher, St. Enda, was the resort of all the best minds in Ireland. The school at Clonfert was planted by St. Brendan the Voyager, whose reputed travels, under the title of *Navigatio Brendani*, were known throughout mediaeval Europe; it was the seat of St. Fursa (whose account of his Visions excited so wide an interest at one time that it has been held they offered suggestions even to the author of the *Divine Comedy*), and of the illustrious St. Cummian, some of whose writings are still extant, and who wins the admiration of the modern scholar by his intellectual humility and by the vastness of his learning. Clonmacnoise, now a desolate ruin in a lonely countryside, was founded by St. Kieran, and his cell soon became the centre of a veritable city of students. Iniscaltra became so famous for its school and monastery that an old record recounts how on one day there entered the mouth of the Shannon seven ships, full of students from foreign parts, bound for that little island on Lough Derg.

Aspirants, eager to gain and to bring back to their own darker homes the light of Western wisdom, came from all and sundry regions of Europe. Dagobert, a king of France, Aldfrid, king of Northumbria, St. Willibrord, a Saxon noble, afterwards Archbishop of Utrecht, Agilbert, a Frank, and afterwards Bishop of Paris, were among those educated at Irish schools. The Venerable Bede mentions that crowds of Anglo-Saxons went over to study in Ireland, where he reports they were kindly received and, without payment, were provided with books and with instruction. Aldhelm, abbot of Malmesbury, records that, while Canterbury School was not over-full, the English swarmed like bees to the schools in Ireland. Visitors came too, it is said, from Gaul,

Germany, Italy, and even from Egypt.

Nor was this intellectual traffic one-sided. Irish saints and scholars went out from their homeland diffusing their knowledge and leaving behind them in Europe traces which remain to this day. St. Columbanus and St. Gall, of the school at Bangor on Belfast Lough evangelised parts of Burgundy, Lombardy, and Switzerland. Dungal, from the same school, was a friend of Charlemagne and was the founder of the University of Padua. St. Aidan, of Galway, at the invitation of Oswald, King of Northumberland, went over to help in the conversion of the king's subjects to Christianity, and founded the monastery of Lindisfarne. He was the first in the line of Bishops to take their title from Durham. His successor was Saint Finan of Tipperary, whose efforts (with those of two other Irishmen, Cedd and Diuma) carried the Gospel far down into Central England. Fergil, or Virgilius, became Archbishop of Salisbury. St. Fursa worked for six years as missionary in East Anglia, and then went over to France, where he earned a wide reputation for virtue and learning. St. Finbar of Connacht aided in the conversion of Mercia, and developed the monastery of Glastonbury. It is said that to-day 155 Irish saints are still venerated in Germany, 46 in France, 32 in Belgium, 13 in Italy, 8 in Denmark, Norway and Sweden.

Those who thus found in Ireland a fountain of knowledge at which they could slake their thirst were not unappreciative beneficiaries; sometimes an old record will give some quaint witness to the gratitude of eminent foreigners to the Irish schools which had taught them so well.

Thus there is still extant a letter from Alcuin, the most learned man at the court of King Charles of France, addressed in affectionate terms to "his blessed master and pious father" Colcu, or Colgan, chief Professor at Clonmacnoise. Not only did Alcuin send a letter, but he sent also 100 shekels of silver (50 from himself and 50 from the king) to the brotherhood of Clonmacnoise as a gift, with a quantity of olive oil for the Irish Bishops.

For a time fate rang down the curtain upon this scene of intellectual activity and happiness. The Danes arrived, terrorising and destroying. Invasion followed invasion. But when in A.D. 1014

Brian Boru utterly defeated the Danes at the battle of Clontarf and set the land free, missionary work was again resumed. This was the period when Irish influence in Germany was at its height.

A monk from Donegal founded a monastery of St. James at Regensburg in 1076. Soon a daughter house was opened at the same place, dedicated to St. Jacob. From this centre Irish influence spread in all directions. Twelve Irish monasteries were founded in Germany and in Austria, at Wurzburg, Nurnburg, Constanz, Vienna, Eichstadt, and other places. Irishmen coming directly from their native land travelled far and wide through Europe carrying the Gospel, and sometimes founding monasteries. Irishmen were chaplains of Conrad III and of Frederic Barbarossa. Under the latter monarch a monastery was founded in what is now Bulgaria, and an Irishman appointed abbot. John, Bishop of Mecklenburg, preached to the Vandals between the Elbe and the Vistula. Pope Adrian IV studied under an Irish professor in the University of Paris. The fame of Irish saintliness and learning was established everywhere. Students still came, like their ancestors, to visit this island so celebrated for its intellectual and spiritual wealth.

But this revival burnt itself out, and no such flame has ever since been lit again. With the Normans there was introduced a condition of permanent warfare, which soon disintegrated Irish life. Suitable recruits were no longer sent out to the Continent, and the great Irish monasteries in Germany and elsewhere were either secularised, like that at Nurnburg, or turned over to local authorities, like those at Vienna or Wurzburg.

Such, in brief, were the Christian schools, such the signal achievement which won for Ireland that title which remains unforgotten as a call to aspiration, showing that once she has been, and yet may be again, an island of saints and scholars.

Long years of invasion and turmoil followed, but the settlers who came in this period to Ireland from overseas did not obliterate this temperamental mysticism of the native race. Indeed, in the era of Plantation it was noted that they soon took on the general characteristics of the people they had come to dwell among and became "more Irish than the Irish themselves."

Early in the eighteenth century, as if to prove that the flame of mystical genius, if overlaid, still burned in Ireland as strong as ever, there arose George Berkeley, Bishop of Coyne, whose spirit of self-sacrifice and missionary enthusiasm made him own brother of the ancient Irish saints. He foresaw the future greatness of America and in his verses *On the Prospect of Planting Arts* and *Learning in America* wrote the famous lines:

> "Westward the course of empire takes its way.
>   The first four acts already past
>   A fifth shall close the drama with the day—
>   Time's noblest offspring in his last."

He conceived the project of founding a college in the Bermudas by a charter from the crown for the Christian civilisation of America, and managed to get a vote of £20,000 from the English House of Commons for the purpose. In 1728, he sailed west and for three years—by way of preparation for Bermuda—lived and laboured in Rhode Island. As the promised grant was withdrawn he was obliged to return to Ireland, but not before he had planted in America the seeds of his idealistic philosophy. Westward therefore as well as eastward the missionary light of Irish Christianity has shone! Berkeley's place in history, however, is due to his metaphysical insight. His famous and often misunderstood doctrine of the non-existence of matter means in reality that matter apart from its apprehension by mind—the mind of man or the mind of God—has no existence at all. In other words, he held, (it has been said) that the material universe can have no existence apart from its inclusion in a great spiritual order, which one may call the life of God. Since his day, illustrious critics have variously challenged, ridiculed, pondered over, commended, admitted the validity or exposed the fallacy of his arguments; but they have not ignored his philosophy. "It is a fact of history," writes one authority, "that Berkeley has employed the modern philosophical world in a struggle, virtually about his new conception of the Universe, which has lasted for nearly two hundred years." Primate Darcy, in a sermon on Berkeley in which he quoted from a number of contemporary philosophers, concluded "My purpose in referring to these works of to-day, the writings of men who occupy a foremost position in the world of thought in our time, is to show that the influence of Berkeley in philosophic thought at the present time is more potent and more creative than at any time in the past. Philosophy cannot get away from him."

Berkeley died in 1753, a true successor of the saints and scholars of old and perhaps the only Irishman who has earned an assured place in the main current of world thought.

Now once again—among the manifold activities of the nine-teenth-twentieth centuries—Ireland has given conspicuous expres-sion to this same spiritual gift in a new form. "A man is hidden behind his tongue," says an Arabian proverb. A nation is hidden behind its literature. The writings of a people form a mirror in which the popular mind and heart are reflected. A poet is not a creator only, but a revealer; and he reveals, not only his own soul, but the soul of his people and of his age. The recent revival of letters in Ireland has been written about in many lands as an Irish Renaissance. And in the work of this Renaissance no human quality has found such general or such felicitous and ardent expression as that of spirituality.

In all ages nations have been proud of their poets. When they wish to display their greatness, it is to their poets they point—the English to Shakespeare, the Germans to Goethe, the Italians to Dante, just as long ago the Romans pointed to Vergil and the Greeks to Homer. A country's poets give the highest expression of the national character. Set half-a-dozen poets of the Irish Revival beside a similar group of to-day's poets from England, or the Colonies, or from America, and one of the traits which is seen at once to mark the Irish writers is the vividness and ardour of their religious feeling. This feeling is not, of course, absent from the contemporary poets of other lands: far from it. But it is not else-where so pervasive, so emphatic, as in Irish verse, nor has it the same quality of instinctive yearning and aspiration. No one can read the verse of Lionel Johnson, of Katharine Tynan-Hinkson, of Pearse, of Dora Sigerson, of Joseph Campbell in his earlier years, or of many another, without noting the devotional and often mystical quality of the author's temperament. Indeed, the wealth of idealistic material is so great that it is some matter of surprise that no one has yet published an anthology of Irish verse of this special type.

The two finest and most famous of Irish poets are, however, those in whose works this spirituality shines out with the greatest brilliance and power. It is to both Yeats and A.E. the one dominant thought, the one central theme. The hero of their verse is not man the mortal, but man the immortal, and their sadness is that of a spirit ill-content to dwell in a house of clay amid a world of illusions. Yeats has spoken of "the disembodied ecstasy" of A.E.'s verse, and no two words can better describe its special quality. "Be it thine," writes A.E. of his own poetry, "be it thine to win Rare vistas of white light, Half-parted lips through which the infinite murmurs its ancient story . . . until thy song's elation Echoes the multitudinous meditation." His verse is, in an extraordinary degree, aetherial, and its ideals of human life noble and august. He loves his country, but has no patience with those who are slaves of the embittering traditions of history. Of himself and those who think like him he says:

> "We are less children of this clime
> Than of some nation yet unborn,
> Or empire in the womb of time.
> We hold the Ireland in the heart
> More than the land our eyes have seen,
> And love the goal for which we start
> More than the tale of what has been.
> We would no Irish sign efface,
> But yet our lips would gladlier hail
> The first-born of the coming Race
> Than the last splendour of the Gael.
> No blazoned banner we unfold,
> One charge alone we give to youth,
> Against the sceptred myth to hold
> The golden heresy of truth."

If only the voters of Ireland could reach up to this thought, how quickly might the ship of State sail out from among the rocks that now beset us, and seem likely to beset out children!

A.E. looks out upon a world full of unhappiness, and he sees human sorrow as springing always from men's forgetfulness of their divine origin and of that high estate which once was theirs before they descended into this world of matter. "We dwindle down beneath the skies, and from ourselves we pass away." They who forget they are from everlasting spiritual beings invoke misery. The remembrance of this truth brings an inward joy which lies "far beyond earth's misery" and is the one road to real dominion and self-completion. Lesser goals of effort than this delude and disappoint. The whole universe, in its vastness and in its tiniest detail, is spirit-woven, and the Mighty Artist who reared "the changing halls of day and night" shows forth His delight likewise in the perfection of the wild flower of the field.

The volume of his *Collected Poems*, first published in 1913, and many times reprinted, includes more than two hundred and thirty pieces, and runs to 369 pages. The treatment of a theme so vast and rich in so many brief lyrics leaves, perhaps, on the reader a sense of fragmentariness. More than twenty years ago a writer in an American paper, the *Sewanee Review*, spoke of A.E. as an "Irish Emerson." It is a suggestive comparison; but Emerson was a dreamer and a thinker, while A.E., in his verse, appears rather as a dreamer and a singer. The view of life and of the universe which A.E. presents is taken from the Upanishads. The mythology which he employs is Celtic. Those readers, therefore, who are trained in the classical tradition of the West may find themselves here in a strange world. But the poet's facility, the splendour of his language, the delicacy of his colour-sense, the occasional magic of his descriptive phrases, attract and charm; and no reader can be unmoved by the magnanimity and loftiness of the poet's thought. Technically the work does not always show infallible clarity and finish. The poet seems a genius first, an artist in the second place. Yeats, on the other hand, is a genius in the second place, an artist first.

If Mr. Yeats has not in the same degree as A.E. an unquenched and unquenchable assurance of the truth and reality of his vision, nevertheless his work likewise depends for its individuality on a rare and ardent idealism. The dominant mood of his poetry, taken as a whole, is one of dream and reverie, of loneliness and longing. A belief in something better than the actual and a desire to reach and to enjoy it, form the main source of his inspiration. And though he has written in many moods, and ranged far in his choice of themes, yet it is when he makes adoration his motive that his touch is most sure, his eloquence most compelling. His idealism has many sides, and the ideal types which his heart or fancy present to him are now of one kind, now of another. Sometimes it is an image of ideal love on which he broods, sometimes an image of ideal joy, sometimes of ideal beauty. But the one of which he dreams more constantly than any other, the ideal of which he writes with a reiteration that never seems to slacken or grow weary is a perfection of beauty—a beauty still sensuous yet transcendently more fair than any that charms the senses of mankind on earth.

With the world of ethics his idealism has little concern. Save in one brilliant poem, he pays scant attention to perfection of character or to standards of conduct. He has shown in the *Countess Cathleen* what he can do in this field when he so wills. He has here taken an old legend which tells how once upon a time an Irish Princess, in order to save her people, gave up for them the most precious thing she possessed, her own soul. When she died, the Almighty pardoned her and received her into heaven because, if her deed was evil, her motive was divine. This story Mr. Yeats weaves into a dramatic poem, in which he does not bring out the conflict of the warring forces within the heroine's breast before she makes her awful decision, but emphasises the moral beauty of her act and the religious significance of her ultimate forgiveness. The Lady Cathleen seems not so much a mere being of the earth as the spirit of a selfless love incarnate in a woman's form. The whole poem is of so high and rare a loveliness that none of Mr. Yeats's later work, brilliant though it be, seems quite to fulfil the promise given here.

Joy is set by the poet among his ideals, and yet it plays but a small part in his poetry. He writes with more affection of sorrow; and the lady of his dreams is nearly always sorrowful, and never joyous. He speaks of joy as one of the marks of the land of his heart's desire, and in the *Wanderings of Oisin* he tells in a score of graceful lines the part joy plays in the universe. But even here, when he sings joy's praise, he carries little conviction, because he sings always in a minor key. Nor does Yeats write of the love of man and woman with the enthusiasm that marks most poets, and which inspires them to their best verse. Only in one poem does he tell what is essentially a love story, or seek to express that inspiration which impels the soul to seek for happiness through a love union with its perfect mate. But here, in *Shadowy Waters* (which, though in form dramatic, is in its nature lyric and personal) the theme has done for Mr. Yeats what it has done for almost every poet who has treated it—it has ennobled his style and enabled him to write some of his most exquisite and haunting poetry. Apart from this poem, Mr. Yeats's attitude toward love is one of deprecation. As implied in many places and expressed in his *Rose of Battle*, his view is that love brings contentment and repose which are inimical to the divine hunger of the poet. It is to the sad, the lonely, the insatiable, that Nature reveals her mysteries. The poet must abjure love and drive it from him to "hide its face amid a crowd of stars."

Doubtless the poet's failure to write at length of joy and love and moral perfection is not so much due to his loving these less, but to his loving another ideal even more. The ideal which he prizes most highly is that of beauty. He chants the praise of beauty in his lyrics, his narratives, his plays. He chanted it when he was a boy, and he chants it now he is a man. So active is his imagination when enkindled by the desire for beauty, that the poet seems able to look at his ideal now from this angle, now from that, to see it in a hundred different forms, and to sing it in a hundred different ways. And if he writes of this theme late and early, he writes of it also with an emotion which, though it may seldom be impassioned or rapturous, is always sincere and earnest and profound.

The great function of poetry is to him the expression of beauty. He sees the poets as "labouring all their days to build a perfect beauty in rhyme." Nor could they well choose a worthier theme, since it is the love of beauty that has impelled men to the heights of epic achievement (as in old Hellas and ancient Ireland). Moreover, beauty was, indeed, the cause of creation, since God made the world that He might provide the Angel of Beauty with a place where she might wander at will. In one poem Mr. Yeats claims that an aesthetic difference is an ethical one, and that ugliness is unrighteous. "The wrong of unshapely things," he cries, "is a wrong too great to be told." So monotheistic is he in his worship that when he turns to indite a poem in honour of Erin he fears he may be guilty of unfaithfulness, and, therefore, saves himself by propounding the belief that beauty is the tutelary Goddess of Erin, and still loves that land as her peculiar haven and home on earth. In what might seem intended as love poems Mr. Yeats writes not so much of love as of beauty. He praises his beloved because she reminds him of the loveliness that has long faded from the world; he tells her that when she sighs, he hears White Beauty sighing too, and that she seems to him an incarnation of that Angel of Beauty to whom his heart is given. He does not seem self-forgetful, like the true lover, but conscious of himself and of his dreams; so that, for instance, when he tells his beloved that he spreads before her feet his dreams as cloths for her to walk upon, he is careful to ask that she tread lightly.

This sensuous beauty, which Yeats so devoutly adores, he often personifies as a woman or goddess of whom he is the humble devotee and priest. But at other times he thinks rather of some ideal age or place where there is nothing, neither form nor colour, nor odour, nor sound, that is not beautiful. Frequently he speaks of bygone ages as possessed of a loveliness which, like Astraea, has long since fled from earth. In one or two brief lyrics some favourite spot in Ireland like the Lake Isle of Innisfree is painted as the ideal place of his dreams. But in his larger works the dwelling-place and home of beauty is some imaginary land beyond the known borders of the world—in *The Wanderings of Oisin* it is the Isle of the Blessed; in *The Land of Heart's Desire* it is the realms of Faery; in *Where There is Nothing* it is the heaven of the mystic's faith.

It has been Mr. Yeats's custom to place this halcyon home of

Beauty in strong and striking contrast to the actual life of man on earth. The workaday world he shows as a hard and sordid place, whose darkness he uses as a foil to set off the glory of the land of his dreams. This opposition is, to him, not a mere artistic device, but a profound fact of Nature, and it provides him with the subject of some of his best poetry. Indeed, the poems which have appealed to his readers as most sincere, and which are the most general favourites, are precisely those in which this opposition is the crux and central theme.

In these points Mr. Yeats's method—if without injustice to his art one may point for a moment to the foundations and the ground-plan on which he has built—is to place the hero (or heroine) in the midst, with Earth on one side and Elysium on the other, and then have him decide which of the two he will choose. The making of the choice, the struggle to escape from earth, and the final attainment of Elysium provide the plot. The hero's weariness of earth, his longing for Paradise, and his delight on reaching his haven, supply the emotion of the piece. Names, dates, places may vary, but this plan varies not. Oisin, Maire Bruin, Forgael, Paul Rutledge—mythic warrior, peasant girl, pirate, and nineteenth-century country gentleman—all stand in similar dilemmas, all make a similar election, and all reach similar goals. There is, however, one play which, though it belongs to this class, yet stands by itself as apart from its fellows. This is *Cathleen Ny Houlihan*. For in this piece the hero does not seek the personal enjoyment of any delectable Paradise, but refuses the good things of earth that he may the better do his duty and fight in his country's cause.

Yet if in this large group of poems Mr. Yeats changes neither the theme nor the essentials of his plot, he does considerably change his point of view and his treatment of the story. When he was young he looked at the matter from one angle, and wrote *The Wanderings of Oisin;* when he was a little less young, his point of view was changed, and he wrote *The Land of Heart's Desire;* when he reached middle age he saw it all in yet another way, and wrote *Where There is Nothing*. In his youth his fancy broke its leash, and he revelled in the delights of his dream-

Elysium. His hero of this period, Oisin, escapes forthright from earth and rides with a fairy bride to the Isle of the Blessed, and the poet fills almost the whole of his poem with enraptured descriptions of that wonderful world. But with growing experience Mr. Yeats's perspective changed, and the thought of earth became obtrusive. Maire Bruin, the main figure in *The Land of Heart's Desire*, did not find so quick or easy an escape to the place of her dreams as did Oisin. It is only when Earth has grown at last unbearable that she calls for the fairies, whom she has loved so long, to take her out of "this dull world." Even then her decision has to be fought out in a hard and bitter struggle, for earth has its ties, and she cannot win her fairy land till she has broken the bonds of faith and home. Paul Rutledge has a yet more arduous experience than Maire. Less fortunate than she, he does not know where that which he desires is to be found. No fairy-child, no princess from the Happy Isles, comes to his need. He must go out and search for his ideal himself. He does so in a fashion which is, at least, uncompromising, and becomes by turn tinker, monk, and self-appointed friar. But his goal remains unknown till, at the very last, as he drops dying beneath the stones of the mob, he cries "I go to the sacred heart of flame," and finds his soul's desire through martyrdom. So hardly did Paul Rutledge attain what Oisin was given as a gift; and so little is the reader told of that Paradise which in the earlier poem a thousand glowing lines were hardly sufficient to describe.

Mr. Yeats himself is acutely conscious of this change. He sees no more the heavens opened, nor does he tell burning tales of dream-guided adventurers forsaking all to seek the mystic home of Beauty. He cannot write now in that high, happy strain. His songs no more thrill with faith and hope. He doubts. "Is this my dream, or the truth?" he asks. Once he wrote a poem—*The Rose of the World*—to protest against the false dream that "Beauty passes like a dream." Now he records the wisdom of the old men: "I heard the old, old men say, 'All that's beautiful drifts away like the waters.'" He feels the loss and laments the change. "I am worn out with dreams," he cries; and again, "Now my heart is sore. All's changed"—"My barren thoughts have chilled me to the bone"—and

> "The holy centaurs of the hills are vanished;
> I have nothing but the embittered sun;
> Banished heroic mother moon and vanished,
> And now that I have come to fifty years
> I must endure the timid sun."

He tries to think, however, that if the fading of his early vision be sad, yet it has its gains. Perhaps he was wrong then and is right now.

> "Through all the lying days of my youth
> I swayed my leaves and flowers in the sun;
> Now I may wither into the truth."

"The truth!" What, then is this truth which has come when joy is gone? One reads *The Green Helmet,* and comes on the following lines, and wonders whether they really can be written by the same pen as that which charmed all hearts not long ago with a story of that *Land of Heart's Desire* where beauty has no ebb, decay no flood":

> "How shall I know
> That in the blinding light beyond the grave
> We'll find so good a thing as we have lost?
> The hourly kindness, the day's common speech,
> The habitual content of each with each,
> When neither soul nor body has been crossed."

Heaven, it seems, is closed. Only the earth remains. But when the poet took this for the burden of his song, his power and his rapture left him. He is still the craftsman, but he cannot move men's spirits. Like his heroic Oisin, so soon as he slips from his faery-steed and touches the common earth, his strength turns to water and the years master him. "O, who could have foretold that the heart grows old!" he cries. He has no tidings now. What is an Irish poet who has lost his idealism? He is as a saint without the knowledge of heaven, as a scholar without the knowledge of the earth.

But Mr. Yeats has not spoken his last word. Progress moves not in a straight line, but in a spiral. Wordsworth's Child, who at first saw all things apparelled in celestial light, and later, as he grew to man's estate, lost the happiness of this intuitive vision, found in later years the same high wisdom restored and deepened through thought and contemplation. So may it be with this poet whom God has gifted and man has justly honoured. Before he lays down his pen he will, of a surety, see once again the gates of pearl cast wide, and, in fuller, stronger tones than ever before, will sing in his old age the glories of the Land of the Ever-Young.

The poems of Mr. Yeats, with those of A.E., have made the name of Ireland honourably known through the English-speaking world, particularly among the educated and most influential classes. They have, in a dark and doubting age, upheld with power and persuasiveness, the cause of idealism and of spirituality. They have had the effect, throughout the Empire and in America, of connecting this cause with the revival of letters in Ireland. It has been felt that the special qualities of these poems are not merely personal, but are typical of the genius of the Irish people.

Here lies the national significance of these two great poets' work. Their achievement is not the singular and unaccountable outburst of an extraordinary talent; it is not unrelated to its environment, a flaming bush in a wilderness. On the contrary, Mr. Yeats and A.E. are children of their country. Their greatest and most splendid quality is one which they inherit from Ireland. Their power of vision is an Irish gift. It marked the Irish long ago, and it marks them now. What is singular in their attainment is not that they possess the seer's temperament, but that to it they add a rare faculty of poetical expression. It is not their privilege to sing of themes unknown or strange to the Irish people, but rather to give utterance to aspirations which many among the Irish felt, yet none but themselves can put in music or in words. Indeed, what these two men have achieved might well be impossible had they not had the spirit of the people with them. For they have done something which, in the realm of letters, is comparable with the work of an ancient Irish missionary in the realm of religion. In an age when the Philistines have captured the Ark of Beauty, when most poets sing of earthliness and shadows and despair, here are two Irishmen singing, in strains of rapture and desire, tidings of joy and light and loveliness.

> "Men yet shall hear
> The Archangels rolling Satan's empty skull
> Over the mountain tops"

is continually the burden of their song. And where else in the wide world to-day will this be found as the characteristic and dominant note of a nation's contemporary verse?

Perhaps the victory of the Archangels over Satan which Yeats foretold was nearer than he knew. Perhaps had he learned where to turn his ear, he might have found yet fairer songs to sing in his later years than he had found in his brilliant youth.

Our poets saw in vision the eternal light of heaven shining afar and caught a glimmer of its radiance down on this earth amidst the uncomprehending gloom of human life. They expressed their vision in forms and images gathered from the love of the ancient East or from the myths and faery legends of their own land. They did not sing of the Marriage of Heaven and Earth, of the Sun God scattering for ever the Spirit of Darkness, nor—as Shelley did—attempt in a hundred impassioned lyrics to raise the chant of all created things hymning in adoration the glory of a regenerated Universe.

Their imaginations ranged far and wide for thoughts and images through Celtic or mediaeval or oriental myths and legendary lore; they did not seek their inspiration from the one central source from which Columba and his fellow saints and scholars derived their knowledge and their strength.

Now has come, now has spread far and wide through the globe a fuller, richer, happier Message; the Message promised by Christ long ago and now at length after well-nigh two millenniums brought by him and given in tones that are heard only by spiritual ears (as He used to say when He taught "He that hath ears to hear let him hear"). A poet-prophet of the East, a hero-saint of the ancient land of Irán, Bahá'u'lláh, has brought, as God's Messenger, Tidings of a New Heaven and a New Earth. Tidings that Light's Arrows have pierced the heart of Darkness, that the battle which the Patron Saints of Ireland fought of Truth against Error, Knowledge against Ignorance, Love against Hate, has been won for us, and that Victory will descend when men stretch out their eager hands to gather it. Blinded with self-desire, men and nations drain the bitter dregs of disillusion and cannot see what spectral hand holds to their lips the cup of death—cannot see the underlying cause of the world's want and woe is spiritual poverty.

What nation will be the first to behold the vision of truth, the first to declare it? Might not their great tradition call the Irish to this task?

To consider in how marked a degree this precious gift of spirituality has been theirs in the past: to look back at their history and see how the religious genius of the people has over centuries made Ireland a lamp of Faith in a darkened world, directing its light both East and West, to realise that still there burns deep in the heart of the people that ancient fire: to hear to-day in our midst the voice of poets beginning to raise again the strain so long unheard, and chant in the ears of a forgetful world the praise of eternal beauty and eternal truth: thus to watch, to listen, and to reflect is to be filled with hope that Ireland may not be slow to catch the vision of the New Day, of the coming of the Kingdom of God, and that she may do for mankind now such service as she did for the world long ago in the hour of its darkness and its need.

PART II

MEDITATIONS, DEVOTIONS AND POEMS

For a Seeker

I

I HAVE set forth as Thy pilgrim, my Lord; but there are many lands and unknown seas to travel before I approach the threshold of Thy Sacred Shrine.

At every step I am admitted into a new realm, and at the end of each day's wayfaring I pitch my tent in a fresh El Dorado.

What earthly journey could be like this Journey! What adventure like this Adventure! What were the possession of the whole world compared with the joy of this Quest for Thee!

My longing for Thee ever increases. Wonder uplifts me. My heart leaps with exultation, and trembles in awe. This gift of Thine is beyond all my hopes and my imagining. I do not dream now of the shining domes of Thy far-distant sanctuary. I am no longer restless nor impatient. It is enough for me to seek Thee and to seek Thee, day after day.

O my God, my Beloved! Grant me at Thy hand a draught of the Wine of Immortality that I may seek Thee through this world and all Thy hidden worlds for ever and for ever.

2

LORD, I have launched out upon the vast ocean of Search in the barque of Faith. I know that I shall never find Thee unless Thy hand direct me, and the breath of Thy mercy bear me on the way.

I am weak, and the source of strength lies not in me.

Error perpetually wells up in my soul, estranging me from Thee.

Yet, do I seek Thee for ever! Everywhere I find traces of Thee, and I cannot refrain from my seeking. Thy voice echoes in the still recesses of my heart, and my longing for Thee gives me no rest.

O beloved One; my heart is emptied of all save Thee. Leave me not to my loneliness. Breathe Thy Holy Spirit upon me, that I may be borne far away from the world, and approach the threshold of Thy unity.

3

O LORD of love, Giver of Knowledge!

The twilight of Thy dawn breaks upon my soul, and the shadows of illusion flee before the white arrows of Thy Truth.

Slowly knowledge widens. Unfamiliar meanings gleam from familiar things. Hidden chambers of treasure open before the outstretched hand of thought. I feel like a child carried by magic into a far, strange land. Breathless with astonishment, I behold wonders leap into being everywhere in endless variety. But always the way of Truth is love, the key of Truth is love, and Truth's own self is love.

4

O MY Lord!

I have sought Thee all my life, yet I still wander in a chequered world of light and shadow. Oh, lift me at last into the pure splendour of Thy Truth beyond the reach of any darkness that I may behold Thee as Thou art, and live in Thy continual presence evermore.

5

THE darkness changes and pales, but no light breaks. Error grows intolerable, but Truth still is hidden out of sight. I rest not, but I never reach my goal.

Yet, do I not ask anything, but to journey onward and onward. My path is of Thy making, and Thou leadest me on the way. I ask no more, and I desire no more.

E

6

I HAVE left behind me impatience and discontent. I will chafe no more at my lot. I commit myself wholly into Thy hands, for Thou art my guide in the desert, the teacher of my ignorance, the physician of my sickness.

I am a soldier in my King's Army; I have given up my will to Him, and my life is His to dispose of as He may please.

I know not what fate Thou designest for me, nor what work Thou hast ordained for me, nor will I enquire nor seek to know. The task of the day suffices for me, and all the future is Thine.

Little by little Thou trainest me. Little by little Thou changest weakness to strength, doubt to faith, perplexity to understanding. When I am fit to bear the burden Thou wilt lay it on my shoulders. When I am prepared to take the field Thou wilt assign me a place in Thy army of Light. Now I have no other duty than to equip myself for Thy service.

With eagerness and patience, with hope and gratitude I bend to the task of the hour lest when Thy call to battle comes I be found unready.

7

THE task is hard. But I know it has come from Thy hand; therefore it shall be the choice of my mind, and the delight of my heart. I will utter no word of complaint, nor admit a thought of grief. I will follow in the footprints of all those who have sought Thee for love of Thee. I will find in effort my rest and my peace, and out of pain I will wring a hidden joy.

Thus, O Beloved, Whose sweet voice I hear calling me, and still calling me, I will draw near to Thy abode bearing Thee the only gift Thou wilt accept, the only gift I have to offer: the gift of my heart.

8

FOR every void there is a filling, and to every prayer there is an answer.

All tribulation has its ending, and to every seeking there is a finding.

For the weary, rest is waiting, and for the lonely, love.

Therefore will I be content, and will keep a heart at peace. My faith is founded upon Truth, and I will bear witness through every trial to the goodness and mercy of God.

9

ALONE in the darkness before the dawn I repair to Thy shrine, and bow before Thy sacred threshold. In the rapture of communion with Thee, self and the world momentarily fall away. The veil of Thy Beauty is lifted, and the sweetness of Thy Mercy enfolds me . . .

On the far horizon darkness breaks and flees, and through the tracery of leafless boughs I watch the brightening sky. Day calls me hence, and I must leave Thy sanctuary for the roaring city and the busy mart. Grant me, O Lord, Thy continuing presence and protection, that when night brings me back to Thy temple I may not come to Thee in estrangement nor in shame. Vouchsafe me, all the day through, Thy help and strength. Above the babel let me hear Thy Voice. In the turmoil let Thy Peace hold possession of my heart. When I walk among the idols that once I worshipped, let me not heed them nor remember them, being enrapt with utter love of Thee.

10

To Thee now, O Beloved One, the Merciful, I bring my weakness, my consciousness of failure—to Thee I pour out my griefs—to Thee I confide my disappointments; and from my knees I rise leaving behind me all my burdens, freed from every sadness, strengthened by Thy strength, arrayed in faith, seeing Thy sunshine everywhere and desiring to find throughout the day opportunities of proving my gratitude to Thee for Thy abundant gifts.

11

In the growing light of self-knowledge, O God, I stand revealed to myself, and conscience-stricken I come to Thee in horror and contrition. Till now I never recognised the baseness of my state nor suspected the depth of my guilt in Thy eyes.

Fill my heart so full of love that there shall be no room for anger; so full of hope that there shall be no room for fear; so full of radiant joy that sadness may not enter nor approach. Deprive me, O God, of all the world holds dear, and of all that men may offer unto men; bestow on me pain, penury and humiliation if by this means I may be purified of my sin, and freed from these anarchic passions.

Spare me not. But grant me in the end attainment to my Goal: the knowledge of Thy Truth, the blessing of Thy Love.

12

Out of the dark depths of my being there well up continually hateful desires. The Enemy of my life has his stronghold in the dim mysterious background of my consciousness which lies beyond the reach of my will.

Horrid thoughts and impulses assail me unawares, and in weak moments. I struggle, and I will not yield; but I cannot conquer. Legion succeeds legion, and the tumult is endless.

I long for Thee, O my God: for Thy Truth, Thy Glory and Thy Peace. But how can I win my goal while I lie thus open to my foes, and the Evil Principle has its seat within my heart!

In desperate need, in conscious impotence I turn to Thee. Make me anew, O Lord! Leave me not to this monster who harbours within me. Deliver me from this satanic self. Cleanse my whole being, and light within me such a flame of love as will burn darkness and its brood out of my heart for ever.

13

O my Lord, how can I ask to be delivered from these tests and trials that bring me so much suffering and anguish! They come from Thee, awakening me from self-delusion, and revealing my weakness. I stand before Thy Judgment Seat, uncloaked, dishonoured. Horror overwhelms me and abases me. Then at last shame stings me to life, and remorse spurs me to escape from the cause of this misery.

My Lord, I do not shun pain in Thy path. Whatever it cost me, do not permit me to delay on my journey to Thee, nor to turn aside from Thy way. Send me whatever difficulties or suffering my soul shall need to cleanse and purify it utterly of all that is false and wicked. Help me to grow in self-knowledge and wisdom, and to put into practice what I learn, till each weakness is turned into strength, and I pass into the realm of Thy might through the gates of victory.

14

O LORD!

Thy mercy is endless and Thy love cannot be compassed by gratitude or praise or knowledge. I adore Thee ever more and more; I am overwhelmed with wonder and drawn to Thee in longing and rapture. Yet, this lesser self, this narrow I with whom I am involved turns from Thee again and again and breaks away, flouting Thy law in open rebellion. Ashamed and in utter misery I turn back. I do not dare to approach Thee, but kneel far away in a wretched place, an alien. I cannot understand why I fall away from what I truly desire; and I despair of myself. The desolation of loneliness overwhelms me.

But Thou dost not despair of me. Thy forgiveness descends and touches me ere I raise my eyes to look towards Thee. Thy mercy enlightens me. Thy love pours warm hope again into my heart, and Thou leadest me back to walk in the courts of Thy Spiritual Palace.

Yet, of my own strength I cannot make myself an abiding place close to Thee. There lingers in me the foreboding that again I shall stumble and fall away from the sweetness of this communion with Thy love.

O compassionate almighty God, I commit myself in utter humility to Thy boundless mercy, begging Thee to save me (I know not how) from this Horror, and to vouchsafe me that which is my true, my only desire—to attain to Thy Presence, to know and to obey Thy Truth.

15

To Assailing Doubts

I WILL have God or nothing.

I will not accept that which you offer.

I will not seek help from the world, for it passes and has no strength; nor from ambition, for it cannot satisfy; nor from money, for no man has that to sell which I desire.

I have beheld the Truth, and I will not forget it.

I have heard the promise of my Lord, and I will trust my all to it.

You afflict me, but you will not capture my heart.

You are many now, but you will become few. You seem strong, but your strength is already passing away. You are God's enemies, liars against the Truth, and I am girded with God's strength to master and subdue you. I will not cease from this battle till I have used you that you will never raise your heads from the dust to threaten me again.

16

O GOD!

Help me to give battle to the Enemy, and cease not; but ever to keep my heart in peace.

Help me to be the servant of my fellow servants, and to find in this servitude infinite freedom.

Help me to turn away from the semblance of beauty which lies about me, and to seek in my heart the eternal beauty.

Help me to pass beyond love and hate that in self-abandonment I may cast myself at the feet of the Lord of Joy.   Amen.

17

KEEP Thou, O God, the door of my heart that no evil thought proceed from it; and guard my lips that they utter no uncharitable word.

Teach me to look for the good in others that I may rejoice in it; and for the evil in myself that I may amend it.

Watch over my actions that I do no injustice, nor cause unhappiness to any one.

Divest me of pride that I may count myself less than any other, and may become the servant of all for love of Thee, my Lord.

18

DEAR God of Splendour, Whose light is greater than my darkness, and Whose love is stronger than my loneliness, end forever with one shaft from the Bow of Thy Glory this night of error wherein I wander and am lost.

Light in my heart the fires of love, O God, that being delivered from all self-centred desire I may love Thee for Thine own sole sake without hope of reward here or hereafter, or thought of any heaven save this enraptured abandonment of love for Thee.

19

MAKE my heart, O God, as this unshadowed mountain lake that sets its face forever toward heaven, and in its calm depths reflects the peace of Thy remote vast worlds of light.

20

A Vision of God's Triumph

OUT of the depths I greet the sunlit heights. Out of gross darkness I sing hymns of light.

Thy Glory has spread across the heavens, Thy Beauty has kissed the mountain tops, and Thy Love beats upon the hearts of men.

The doom of the Night has sounded. The troops of darkness gather in the valleys. The stars have fallen. The skies are cleft asunder, and far in the empyrean from the Fountain of Knowledge pours the river of life, and the hosts of heaven chant the Glory and the Victory of God.

The peoples tremble in their sleep. The nations are shaken to their base.

The gates of Hell pour forth the last of their legions.

Where can the Night flee, or the armies of Satan take refuge? Death descends upon them. Despair hardens their hearts. Breathing destruction they are themselves destroyed.

For the Glory of God has encircled the world. His love has filled the earth. The treasure chambers of heaven are thrown wide, and the gifts of the Most High are showered upon Mankind.

There shall be no more death nor oppression nor tears. God has ascended His throne. He has taken possession of the hearts of men.

Therefore from the darkness with hymns of light I greet the Source of Light, and from the depths give answer to the heights.

21

A Vision of the Day of Judgment

ONE touched my eyes. I looked and saw above the Mountain of Holiness the light break. And a Voice above the Mountain called to me and said:

"That thou seest is the Dawning of the Judgment. Therefore, repent, lest thou be found among the workers of inquity.

"Woe to them that have thought to hide their evil deeds in the gloom of their misbelief, and to keep their wickedness secret from their Lord.

"Woe to them who through My long forbearance have imagined Me forgetful, and ignorant of their guilt.

"Woe to the oppressors, and to them that wrong the poor, though it be in ever so little.

"Woe to them that have made My Holy Name a cloak for injustice, and have stamped on My Truth the image of their own base desire.

"Woe to them that misguide My people, reviling My Messengers and traducing My Gifts.

"Woe to them that lift their strength against My strength, and utter blasphemy against My Word.

"Woe to them that turn away from My Light, and seek the shelter of the darkness.

"Their hour is come, and the Seal of My Covenant is set upon their doom."

The Voice ceased. I watched the dawn grow clear, and the risen Sun pour its beams from the east to the uttermost west, paling the last lone star of morning. The glory of the light ran burning through the sky. At its caress the hidden beauty of the world came forth unveiled. The air instinct with fire trembled in ecstasy. The winds, the seas joining in nature's hymeneal joy chanted the bridal song of Earth and Heaven.

But man, afar, alone, lay unaware, dreaming of vanities, drugged in sleep.

22

Joy is from Eternity!

Joy is more ancient than Time—vast as infinitude!

Out of joy doth all proceed, and in the arms of joy is Creation upheld!

Joy is in the Beginning, Joy is before the founding of the worlds!

Joy is the mighty, the impregnable, the everlasting.

Joy is the life and light of all; and naught exists that is not filled with the breath of joy.

The voice of joy breaks forth on every hand in water, in wind, in rustling leaf and singing bird; and listening night lays her hand upon the earth's wild heart to hear the universal chant of joy float from the fiery stars.

O God, O God, the dawn of joy is broken!

The flood-gates of light are open, and joy descends in torrents on the earth.

The frosts of life melt in the sunshine of Thy joy. Thy kiss of joy has touched all, sweetened all!

Thy joy triumphant conquers the heart of man, and in the depth of our being joy awakes.

There is no room for sadness, for doubt. Within, without, joy fills all space, all time, all thought.

The prophet's voice, the lover's heart, proclaim the victory of joy. Far and wide, in every clime, in every land, the soul of man wakens to join at last that triumph-song of praise which for long ages Truth, unheard of men, has sung to God in solitude.

For Ireland

LOOK Thou, O Father, upon this land where once Thy Son's name set hearts on fire and His light shone in lonely splendour across the darkness of the west.

Now in this Advent of a mightier Day awake anew that power of vision, that readiness to answer Thy clear call. Make us on whom the fullness of the times has come, prove ourselves true heirs of all that is most heroic in our past. Use once again, but now for a yet larger end, the spiritual gifts Thou hast vouchsafed this people. Let them swiftly arise as one in common acclamation of the Day of Glory.

Thou hast in this Great Age ordained the nations of the west to bear to the world the Message of Thy regeneration of the whole human race. Guide, O Father in heaven, the people of this land to the path Thou hast appointed them. Kindle the flame of adoration in our hearts; teach us the joy of the soul's surrender to its God. Speed us on our forward way. In our share of service to this crowning Day of Days let us find at last the challenge and the meaning of our country's ancient title, Inisfail, the Isle of Destiny.

For Father and Mother

23

O WATCHFUL and loving Lord! Keep our little ones this day under Thy protection. Permit no evil influence to reach or to come near them. Preserve them from illness, from accident, and from all mishap. And in the evening bring them home to their rest in safety and happiness.

24

PRAISE be to Thee, O God, Who hast given to these children the boon of earthly life, and brought them thus far upon the road that leads to life eternal!

O Thou of many gifts, vouchsafe these little ones the mortal boon of health, prosperity and happiness; and since these blessings soon must pass away and be no more, admit them to Thy boundless worlds of love, endow and so train their hearts that they may be able to receive and hold fast for ever in joy the knowledge of Thy coming and Thy glory. Thou art the All-Compassionate, the All-Wise.

25

THIS home is a garden, O Lord, which Thy hand has planted in the world, and the hearts of these children are Thy flowers. Do Thou tend them and nourish them.

Pour down the rays of Thy truth upon them. Breathe Thy Holy Spirit upon them at every breath. Let Thy mercy descend on them like refreshing rain.

So shall these flowers of Thine mature, and bloom in beauty, and shed afar the fragrance of Thy love and remain thine to their lives' end.

26

PRAISE be to Thee, dear Lord, Who grantest to Thy servants bounty upon bounty. Thou bestowest on us the marriage-blessing of children bringing with them a thousand delights; and in this very gift Thou openest to us of Thy grace a new world of service to Thee, a new road to Thy good pleasure and favour.

Help us, in love and gratitude to Thee, so to direct and train these little ones that they may become men and women after Thine own heart, and may take their place as Thy lamps shining brightly in a dark world.

27

O THOU, the Lover, the Creator and the Lord of these children, help us their parents to guard and train them not through human love alone, but as an act of love for Thee, and of obedience to Thy command.

Grant us selflessness and devotion, that we may be able in our hearts to hear Thy bidding, and understand Thy will for these little ones.

Help us to do for them our utmost in Thy name, and in calm trust to leave the rest to Thee, the All-wise Who lovest these Thy children better yet—far better—than any human parent may love his child.

28

LET Reverence towards Thee, dear Lord, and kindness towards all that lives be graven deep into these children's hearts.

Give to us, their parents, wisdom and steadfastness, that we may unfold to them, little by little, at the right time and in the right way, the knowledge of Thy Truth, and by the example of our lives may amend whatever is amiss in our teaching.

Let them increase day by day in spiritual strength that they may learn of Thee the mystery of prayer, and may attain the reward of conscious communion with Thy Spirit.

29

O Father in heaven, Who givest to a parents' intercession a special privilege, hear Thou our prayer for these children whom Thou hast entrusted to our care.

Protect them, we beseech Thee, against the evil that arises in their own hearts, against the contagion of their parents' frailties and imperfections, against the power of those whose hearts are turned from Thee.

Help us to pray for our children with concentration and humility of spirit, and by force of prayer offered in Thy Name to keep back, far from them, the evil influences that seek their destruction.

30

O Thou Who hast blessed us with Thy gift of children, let not the wonder and the happiness of these days of their infancy ever pass wholly from our hearts!

Grant us a strong undying memory of whatever is most precious in these fleeting days, that in the aftertime when our little ones are no longer little we may still keep in our hearts countless images and echoes of their babyhood, may see again their open innocent faces, may hear their voices striving to imitate their elders' speech and recall these tireless infant feats of growing knowledge and gathering strength.

So shall the unworldly beauty of these childhood days abide with us forever, and not be wholly lost in the ripe happiness of the later time.

31

"Of such is the Kingdom of Heaven."

GRANT to these little ones, O Lord, that the gifts and qualities which now are theirs through weakness they may make their own by strength. Let them through all the years retain this child-like heart, continuing humble and receptive as now, full of wonder, eager to learn. Increase day by day and year by year their faith that as the children of a Higher Home than this they may become heirs of Eternity and earn the blessed fruits of this Divine Age of Fulfilment.   Amen.

32

HERE, O Lord, within the precincts of Thy protection, Love is king and Faith and Hope are the lords of thought. But in the world without, Faith and Hope wander in a wilderness and a stranger sits upon Love's throne.

Be Thou, O Lord, the strength and shield of these little ones from their life's beginning to its very end. Grant that their love and faith and hope may prevail against every enemy and put to shame all doubt and disbelief. Give them fortitude and power that through childhood and manhood, in prosperity and in adversity, they may continue that journey toward Thee which here they have begun, and may to their lives' end bear witness to Thy truth and remain firm in Thy covenant.

33

O GOD, look on us who with ceaseless care keep watch and ward over these children, and suffer not our anxiety for them to become a sign of lack of trust in Thee.

We acknowledge that they are in Thy safe keeping. It is for Thee to appoint unto them their tasks in life, and Thou wilt bestow on them ample strength and means to perform all that Thou requirest.

Help us to pass on to them the divine Message of the Day of God to give to them the best we have to give, and doing this, to leave their souls to Thee in perfect trust.

34

PRAISE be to Thee, O God, for Thy bounty to the weak, the young, the humble, and for Thy power whereby Thou doest whatsoever Thou willest, unhelped, unhindered, uncomprehended by the thoughts of men!

Thou puttest down the mighty, and dost exalt them of low estate.

Thou hidest Thy mystery from the wise and learned, and revealest it to them who are as babes.

The scholar and philosopher see and perceive not, read and understand not; the child beholding Thy beauty steps into Thy Kingdom.

O Loving Lord, Who hast never turned away from a longing heart, nor an appealing cry, we pray then by Thy Most Great Name to deal with these little ones—these tender branches of the tree of life—according to Thy all perfect knowledge and desire.

35

O LORD, look upon these little ones, children of Thy covenant born of those whose hearts are turned to Thee. Keep them from the first unto the last under Thy protection and suffer them not to follow any desire save what may become servants of Thy truth, lovers of Thy Beauty.

36

HEAR Thou, O God, our prayer for the children of this Age throughout the world!

Look with pity on those whose parents have not turned their hearts to Thee nor humbled themselves before Thy Manifestation. By Thy boundless mercy and Thy prevailing will, deliver them out of the darkness that surrounds them, and draw them toward Thy light. Create in their souls a hunger and thirst for righteousness, a longing for spiritual truth; and prepare their minds to listen for Thy voice and to welcome Thy glad tidings.

And now, O God, we beg Thee for these our children and for all others born beneath Thy covenant that Thou wilt endow them with power to recognise and to use to the utmost the blessing Thou hast given them. Grant them strength to stand fast by Thy truth, to uphold Thy cause, and in their time to spread far and near the knowledge of Thy glory and dominion.

37

FATHER of mine, and of my little son who kneels at my side and lifts his voice to Thee, hear Thou his prayer and mine. Protect those whom he loves and prays for. Lead him onward and ever onward in Thy way till he shall understand that within his weak and mortal body is hidden the sacred light of Thine imperishable Presence.

38

O TRANSCENDENT and Incomparable Lord!

Thou hast bidden us look to Thee as to our Father in heaven; teach me to keep in my heart this chosen Name of Thine, that I may discern the true ideal of fatherhood, and learn what Thou wouldst have an earthly father be. Strengthen me with Thy Spirit that I may deserve the trust, the obedience and the love of my little ones. Make me remember that they will learn the meaning of fatherhood from their earthly father, and forbid, O Lord, that I by my unworthiness should lead Thy children astray in their first thoughts of Thee. Thou art the Everpresent, the All-wise.

39

THERE was one who, being crossed, spoke to his son in anger, and saw the child's face change in fear.

Thereafter, praying in penitence, he heard the Voice of the Spirit speak to him:

"Think not to number this weak one among thy possessions, nor imagine him to be thy creation. Thou callest him thy son. Yet within his infant soul lies hidden that which is deeper than thy knowing. In heaven his spirit stands now among the angels of My presence, and here on earth the sword of My justice protects and avenges him against all, and especially against thee. Love thou thy son, and love thyself in him. Teach him My way, and walk in it thyself that thou mayest be his guide. He is not thine, but Mine. Therefore, in all thou dost with him keep Me in remembrance, and fear Me. This is thy duty. See that thou fulfil it always, and slack not therein."

40

O LOVING Lord!

To the mountain-stream Thou hast given its bubbles that dance and tremble and break in light.

To the forest depths Thou hast given the fresh flowerbuds that burst and open and unfold their tender petals in perfect beauty.

To me Thou hast given the first baby-kiss of this little one who presses her tiny lips upon my lips in love.

41

LITTLE one, little one of my heart, I am thy first love and the first to give thee a heart in love.

When I come near, thou smilest and stretchest out thy little hands. And when I lift thee to me, thou foldest thine arms about my neck, and pressest thy smooth cheek to mine, calling me love names in thy baby-talk.

What is there so sweet as love! and what love is so sweet as love at its dawning, new love, first love!

Yet night by night I kneel, and beg of Him Who answers every prayer that through the coming years He will make ever more deep and sweet this early love of ours.

42

O LITTLE one, my Una, April's child, thou breath of the spring wind embodied!

The bluebells cluster about thy knees; overhead the giant beech trees spread their half-unfolded leaves; across the meadow the cuckoo calls, and from the distant bog comes the curlew's lonely cry.

How happy art thou, leading the revel of the woods, their native queen, for whom a thousand springs have come and gone to weave thy flower-beauty, and to find their meaning and perfection in these fresh lips and laughing eyes of thine.

O little one, joys more rare than these await thy wakening heart! A richer spring has cast its bounty at thy feet, a greater glory shines from another Heaven. And never morning breaks nor evening falls but lovers' prayers go forth to beg the early vision of God's Golden Age for thee who playest here thinking all happiness is already thine!

43

CHILD of my heart, call not me your Father; and this dear wife of mine that gave you birth, call not her your mother. Think not the home we make for you is your True Home. The life that is bestowed on you through us will soon pass away and perish; but you, my son, you will not perish.

This life is a steed to bear you to the Kingdom of Eternity, of which you are born a Prince. The Ruler of that Kingdom is your Father. His Palace is your Home. You are heir to a mighty princedom because you are born His son.

Ride straight and fast to take your heritage. Fear no danger. Stop not for flood nor foe. Look not to right nor left. Your Father waits for you.

Ride on. Rest not. Remember you are the son of a King.

44

GOOD-BYE, my baby boy, good-bye; you are gone from us for ever!

What love did you bring with you into the world!

What love did you stir and quicken in your father's heart.

With what love have I watched you, played with you, tended you in all conditions, at all hours, by day and by night; and who was happier than I!

How many scenes made beautiful by love, and filled with joy unroll before my eyes. Again I see our child of longing, the first born in his first sleep: the young adventurer voyaging from chair to chair: the blue-clad boy among the buttercups seeking to make playmates of the eluding lambs . . . But all this is past. You are gone from us, my baby-boy, and have no being now save in the close warm strong embrace of your mother's memory and mine.

So must it be.

The bud perishes that the blossom may shed its fragrance, and babyhood yields its place to the larger life of the boy.

And have not you, my little newcomer, my little four-year-old-son, have not you all that the baby who brought you to me had—and how much more. What was all that baby-sweetness of yours which is now gone by save the light you cast before you on your way to me! You too, in your turn, will pass away from me, and the years will ever bring to you change upon change. Deepening happiness awaits you. You will pass from knowledge to knowledge, from strength to strength. And through all the years, you and I, please God, will be the closer friends and comrades because we have loved each other so dearly in the baby-days gone by.

45

WHILE they are at your side, love these little ones to the uttermost. Forget yourself. Serve them; care for them; lavish all your tenderness on them. Value your good fortune while it is with you, and let nothing of the sweetness of their babyhood go unprized. Not for long will you keep the happiness that now lies within your reach. You will not always walk in the sunshine with a little warm, soft hand nestling in each of yours, nor hear little feet pattering beside you, and eager baby voices questioning and prattling of a thousand things with ceaseless excitement. Not always will you see that trusting face upturned to yours, feel those little arms about your neck, and those tender lips pressed upon your cheek, nor will you have that tiny form to kneel beside you, and murmur baby prayers into your ear.

Love them and win their love, and shower on them all the treasures of your heart. Fill up their days with happiness, and share with them their mirth and innocent delights.

Childhood is but for a day. Ere you are aware it will be gone with all its gifts for ever.

46

WE are thy teachers because God has appointed us. You are to hear us because God wishes you to do so. He made us your father and mother, because He chose that you should be taught by us.

We provide you with food and clothing and warmth. This is good; but the good of it will not last forever. The truth we teach you is the greatest of all the gifts we have to give you. Nothing else is important compared with this. Truth and the effects of truth last for ever: not only for a little time. The teaching which God has told us to give you will make you more happy than clothes or houses or pleasure or money. People cannot be happy without truth, even on this earth: in the next world we shall be very unhappy without it.

Remember, these teachings are of more value than all else we have to give you. We teach you because we wish to obey God. We teach you not only because we love you very much, but for God's sake.

To teach you as God would have you taught is not easy. We are not so wise nor so good as we should like to be; nor even so wise and good as we hope soon to become. God himself alone is a perfect teacher. We pray God constantly to help us; and because we so truly wish and strive to please Him He strengthens us with the power and wisdom of His Spirit. Whatever is true in our teaching, and whatever is good and right in it comes not from us, but from God.

47

THE greatest benefit which we have to confer on you is: Guidance to God.

When God chose us to be your parents He commanded us to offer you this guidance. Therefore, it is by His will that we give you His Holy Teaching. We speak to you of Him and of His prophets, we surround you continually with thoughts of faith and worship, and we never cease to pray for you. We cannot compel you to learn the lessons which we teach; we would not compel you if we could, for God intends our wills to be free. You must choose for yourself. Your mother and I are trying—as best we may—to follow the leading of that Guidance, and it is our hope and prayer that you will travel with us. We should be very lonely if we had to take one step without you. For this teaching which God has given us to pass on to you is the most precious thing we have to give you: more precious far than food, or clothes or schooling, or even life itself—for this knowledge is ETERNAL life.

48

FILL Thou, O God, our home with harmony and happiness, with laughter and delight, with radiant kindliness and overflowing joy, that in the union of our hearts Thy love may find a lodging place, and Thou Thyself mayst make this home of ours Thine Own!

49

UNTO Thee, O God, we dedicate this home. Cleanse it from all that is alien to Thee that it may become fit for Thy acceptance, and may be to friend and stranger as to ourselves a place of peace, a refuge from materialism, a herald of Thy Kingdom.

50

O GOD, make Thou this home of ours the garden of affection, a ripening place of love, where the hidden powers of our hearts may unfold, expand and bear the fruit of an abiding joy.

51

GLORY and honour, praise and thanksgiving be unto Thee for ever from us, and from all mankind!

Thou art the One God, the Boundless, the Eternal, Who in Thy creation hast unveiled Thy Majesty and revealed Thy love.

For our sakes Thou hast called from infinitude this realm of space and moulded it to serve the uses of the soul.

For our sakes Thou hast laid upon eternity the semblance of bonds, and measured Time to us with fingers of gold and silver light.

For our sakes Thou hast brought us forth from the void of nothingness, and on the mirror of our being cast the beauty of Thy Own similitude.

52

PRAISE be to Thee Who hast called into being Thy worlds of Time and of Eternity to give utterance to Thy love. Thou hast made all things for man and man for his own glory and blessedness (not for Thine!) In his being Thou hast hidden Thy light; on his heart Thou hast printed Thy image. Thou hast placed the knowledge of Thyself and of Thy heaven before his face, and laid the way thereto plain and open at his feet.

Thou hast commanded from the beginning Thy covenant with man to deliver him from mortality and to grant him the freedom of Thy eternal Kingdom.

Age after age Thou hast sent Thy prophets to renew the same, to bear Thy children love-messages from Thee, and to bestow on them new and ever richer gifts.

Praise be to Thee, O God, from us who remember our benefits, who recount our blessings, and Who from our hearts give thanks unto Thee, the Beloved.

Praise be to Thee Who hast granted us birth in this time of wonder, this great age of breaking light!

We have walked in pride before Thee, but Thou hast overcome us by Thy humility.

We have turned from Thy presence, but Thy love has overtaken us, and drawn us home to Thee.

We have earned the wages of sin, but Thou hast brought to us Eternal Life.

Praise be to Thee Whose compassion has overshadowed us, whose forgiveness has descended upon us, Whose mercy has given us life, Whose hand has guided us to the highway of Thy Kingdom, Who chose for Thyself exile and bonds that Thou mightest redeem us.

O Thou Whose holiness and might are above Thy creatures' praise, accept from us who love and worship Thee this praise we offer.

A Little Child Shall Lead Them

Often with enchanted pleasure
Have I sped an evening's leisure
Taking to me for a guide
From my lonely fireside
Homer or Scheherazade
And the wondrous tales they made
Of a world beyond the dawn
Where magic and her brood were born.
Whoso enters there will meet
Sorceress and grim Afreet
Heroes go adventuring
Carpets fly and sirens sing
Gardens where prodigious gems
Nod on all the flower-stems
Lavish on a beggar's chalice
Wealth that would have decked a palace.
Marvel treads on marvel's heels
Till the dizzy Reason reels
And e'en Fancy is perplexed
Wondering what can happen next
     This I read, and thought it all
Gorgeous but chimerical—
Till the day I married you
And then I found it all was true!
Ghoul and wizard, —— and sprite
Could they all their charms unite
Ne'er should win the witching power
Love has given you for dower.
Though they post on every breeze,
Dive beneath the tropic seas,
Though in cave and mountain peak
Far they roam and long they seek
All they'll win by force of stealth
Were a trifle to the wealth
Of that secret inner world

That within your smile is curled.
      Yours is not a conscious art;
'Tis the wild magic of your heart.
You but speak a simple word
Often said and often heard
When before my wondering eyes
An unveiled Paradise
Bursts about me into flower.
Here each nimble-footed hour
Daft with all the fun that's in it
Dances like a madcap minute.
All the earth in light enfolden
Seems a chamber green and golden
Dight for love's festivities;
And a thousand harmonics
Softer sweeter more endeared
Than my heart had ever heard
Gush from every bank and rise
Fill the woods and touch the skies.
Wind and cloud and leaf and stream
Notes of purest music seem
And all Nature like a choir
Tuned to the sun-God's lyre
In new hymns of jubilee
Chants her ancient ecstasy.
      Yet the flowing cup of bliss
Holds more precious wine than this.
Our sweet rapture did but screen
Brighter glories yet unseen;
'Twas a distant fragrance blown
From a Garden yet unknown.
Love has pierced the mystery
Hid within the prophecy
Of the heavenly poets who said
'By a child shall they be led,'
'From a babe is wisdom gained
From the weak is strength ordained.'

By some mightier miracle
Than any feigne'd charm or spell
A little smiling newborn boy
In his gift will hold more joy
Open glimpses of a heaven
More remote from earth than even
That enchanted land we knew
Where all fairy-tales came true.
Now when e'er I gaze upon
This my loved and loving son,
When beside his bed I keep
Watcho'er his elysian sleep
When I fold him in my arms
Nestling safe from all alarms
Or behold his innocence
With a sinner's reverence—
Lo, an infinite high hope
On my longing 'gins to ope!
With this tiny hand to guide
We will leave the cold earth's side
And faring far and far away
Beyond the springs of night and day
Will travel to the end the road
That bears all lovers up to God.

Envoy

Be of good cheer!
What but the glory of the Light of Light
  Could cast such shadows on a world forlorn?
  If our hearts whispered not the hope of morn
Would we so hate the horror of this night?
What is it else than desperate bitter fear
That drives the troops of evil, who know well
  Their hour is come, to vent their dying rage
  Upon the people of this heaven-lit age
And seek by every means they may to sell
        Their lost dominion dear?

Be of good cheer!
The very depth of our perplexity
  Amid this whirling world of strife and care
  Where disillusion beckons to despair
Is of itself a call for help, a cry
That angels' hearts will not be slow to hear.
For it is ever in such a time as ours,
  When man has ransacked sea and land for rest
  And never sought the heaven in his own breast,
That God reveals once more His hidden powers
        And in His might draws near.

Be of good cheer!
Though all things change, Truth's kingdom is secure.
  The forms of faith come, go, and are forgot,
  But that which they enshrine can perish not.
Altars may crumble, worship will endure.
Those holy things that God bids man revere
Reign on unchecked by man's satanic will;
  Wisdom and love are of a higher birth
  Than these frail phantom forces of the earth
And take their deathless power from Him who still
        Above all change stands clear.

Be of good cheer!
What kings desired in vain God gives to you
  And in this wondrous day before our eyes
  Unseals His ancient book of mysteries
Making all things in earth and heaven new.
Truth hath come down from some far flaming sphere;
Lo, in our midst her sacred fires burn!
  And see—trace back these countless rays of light
  To the One Point wherein they all unite,
And bow your forehead in the dust to learn
  That God Himself is here!

9780853984955